KT-370-375

Index Kitchen Library

Quick and Easy Workday Dinners

TEST KITCHEN PERFECTION

You'll never make a wrong move with a Family Circle® step-by-step cookbook. Our team of home economists has tested and refined the recipes so that you can create fabulous food in your own kitchen. Follow our easy instructions and step-by-step photographs and you'll feel like there is a master chef in the kitchen guiding you every step of the way.

All recipes are double-tested by our team of home economists. When we test our recipes, we rate them for ease of preparation. The following cookery ratings are on the recipes in this book, making them easy to use and understand.

A single Cooking with Confidence symbol indicates a recipe that is simple and generally quick to make—perfect for beginners.

Two symbols indicate the need for just a little more care and a little more time.

Three symbols indicate special dishes that need more investment in time, care and patience—but the results are worth it.

IMPORTANT

Those who might be at risk from the effects of salmonella food poisoning (the elderly, pregnant women, young children and those suffering from immune deficiency diseases) should consult their GP with any concerns about eating raw eggs.

The Publisher thanks: AEG Kitchen Appliances, Liebherr Refrigeration and Wine Cellars; Bertolli Olive Oil; Breville Holdings Pty Ltd; Chief Australia; Kitchen Aid; Sheldon & Hammond.

Front cover: Sichuan chicken, page 78.
Inside front cover: Pork with paprika, potatoes and shallots, page 61.
Back cover: Chicken and leek pies, page 86.

CONTENTS

Top: Lemon grass beef, page 59.
Bottom: Sumac-crusted lamb fillets with baba ganouj, page 30 (left), and Prawns with spicy tamarind sauce page 63 (right).

EASY DINNERS

AFTER A LONG DAY AT WORK, SLAVING OVER A HOT STOVE IS OFTEN THE LAST THING YOU FEEL LIKE DOING. BUT, ARMED WITH A WELL-STOCKED KITCHEN AND THE FOLLOWING IDEAS, YOU'LL HAVE DINNER READY IN NO TIME.

Quick and Easy Workday Dinners offers a selection of evening meals for four people that are quick to prepare, feature a short list of ingredients (readily available from most large supermarkets) and, most importantly, are full of flavour.

This collection has been divided into five chapters for easy reference: Pasta and rice; Grills and barbecues; Pan-fries and stir-fries; Easy stews and casseroles; and Easy bakes and roasts. Meals such as pasta, stir-fries and grills are prepared in under 15 minutes and can be on the table— or in front of the TV—in 30 minutes. Perfect for when you have other plans and have to be out of the house in under an hour. When you have a little more time, stews, casseroles, roasts and bakes (also prepared within 15 minutes) are designed to cook themselves while you relax with the family. These casseroles and stews can also be prepared in advance (allowing time for their flavours to develop) and refrigerated or frozen into serving size portions to be eaten another night—all you'll need to do is reheat and serve.

Organisation is the key to cooking a variety of convenient and tasty workday meals—a pantry well-stocked with staples is a must. 'Pantry staples' are non-perishable products common to many recipes such as flour, canned tomatoes and dried herbs, and those that make versatile accompaniments (rice, pasta and couscous). Restock your pantry when these items are getting low (see suggestions on facing page).

Maintaining a good supply of dry and canned ingredients, oils, herbs and spices is a great start, but let's not forget to replenish the refrigerator with fresh produce—vegetables, dairy products, meat, poultry and seafood. These products have a comparatively short shelf life and must be restocked more often than pantry staples. Fresh ingredients are essential in making up a balanced meal.

Now that the pantry is full and there is a constant supply of fresh ingredients, the weekday cook has the flexibility to plan in advance for the week's meals or to decide on the spur of the moment what's on tonight's dinner menu.

STORE CUPBOARD INGREDIENTS

- beans, canned
- breadcrumbs, dry
- capers
- coconut milk
- couscous
- curry pastes
- flour, plain
- flour, self-raising
- Italian tomato passata, bottled
- mustard (Dijon, wholegrain)
- noodles
- nuts
- oil—it is a good idea to have two types of oil in your pantry at all times; olive oil is good for Mediterranean cooking and salad dressings, while a good all-purpose vegetable or seed oil such as sunflower oil is suitable for general cooking purposes and more compatible to Asian flavours than the distinct flavour of olive oil.
- oyster sauce
- pasta
- polenta
- rice
- salmon, canned
- soy sauce
- spices
- stock (in tetra packs)
- sugar, caster
- sugar, soft brown
- sweet chilli sauce
- tomato paste
- tomatoes, canned
- tuna, canned
- vinegars (balsamic, red wine, white wine, herb infused)

STORAGE

When stored well, packet ingredients should last until their use-by date. Once you have opened packages, remember to seal them properly or store the contents in well-labelled airtight containers.

Check the labels after opening jars of sauces and condiments to ensure they don't require refrigeration after opening. To store pastes (such as tomato and curry) for longer periods of time in convenient small portions, spoon into ice-cube trays, freeze, divide into plastic bags and keep in the freezer until ready to use.

TIME-SAVING TIPS

- Find a good local butcher who pre-dices and slices high-quality meat cuts. This saves not only time but also paying for fat and sinew that you will discard anyway (although take care as some pre-cut meat can be fatty and not at its peak).
- It is handy to have a ready supply of ingredients that are the flavour base for a vast range of meals, in particular garlic, onions, ginger and chillies. Whenever possible, using fresh varieties of these are best as their flavour is far superior to the bottled versions.
- Stocks are a common liquid base to many dishes and, for optimum flavour, it is often recommended to make your own. Good-quality liquid stocks, however, can be purchased and are available in tetra packs or in cans. Canned stocks are available from Asian stores or in the Asian section of most large supermarkets.
- Leftover bread can be made into breadcrumbs—process pieces of bread in a food processor. Store the crumbs in plastic bags in the freezer, ready for use.
- Plan ahead: read through your recipe and get out all the equipment and ingredients that you need, before you start.
- Decide on any side dishes or accompaniments you wish to serve, and where possible, prepare them while cooking the main meal. Many dishes such as stir-fries, curries and pan-fries are accompanied by rice, which takes about 15 minutes to cook. To maximise time usage, start cooking the rice before you start preparing the rest of your meal.

SOUPS AND SALADS

IF YOU FEEL LIKE SOMETHING SIMPLE FOR DINNER, TRY THESE DELICIOUS SALADS AND SOUPS. THEY'RE QUICK TO PREPARE AND TASTE FABULOUS.

TUNA AND CANNELLINI BEAN SALAD

185 g can good-quality tuna in oil, drained (reserving 1 tablespoon oil) • 400 g can cannellini beans, rinsed and drained • 1/2 small red onion, sliced • 1 tablespoon baby capers, rinsed and drained • 100 g semi-dried tomatoes in oil (reserving 2 tablespoons oil) • 75 g baby rocket leaves • 3 tablespoons chopped fresh basil • 1–11/2 tablespoons tarragon vinegar

Toss the tuna, cannellini beans, onion, capers, semi-dried tomatoes, rocket leaves and basil together in a bowl. Whisk the tarragon vinegar and the reserved oils together until well combined, pour over the salad, toss again and season with salt and pepper. Serves 4.

CHICKEN, AVOCADO AND BACON SALAD

2 chicken breast fillets (about 350 g each), trimmed of excess fat • 31/2 tablespoons olive oil • 3 rashers bacon, cut into thin strips • 2 Roma tomatoes, sliced • 110 g mixed lettuce • 1 avocado, cut into slices • 1 tablespoon balsamic vinegar • 50 g shaved Parmesan

Season the chicken well on both sides. Heat 1 tablespoon of the oil in a frying pan and cook the chicken over medium heat for 4–5 minutes on each side, or until golden brown and cooked through. Keep warm. Cook the bacon in the same pan for 4 minutes, or until crisp and golden. Drain on paper towels. Gently toss the tomato, lettuce, avocado and bacon together in a bowl. Cut the chicken on the diagonal into thin slices, then add to the salad. Whisk the vinegar and the remaining oil together until well combined, pour over the salad and toss again. Season. Garnish with Parmesan and serve immediately. Serves 4.

ROASTED VEGETABLE AND HALOUMI SALAD

2 small red capsicums, cut into 3 cm pieces • 2 zucchini, cut on the diagonal into 1 cm slices • 6 slender eggplants, cut on the diagonal into 1 cm slices • 4 Roma tomatoes, cut into quarters • 8 whole cloves garlic, unpeeled • 3 1/2 tablespoons olive oil • 1 tablespoon red wine vinegar • 250 g haloumi cheese, cut into 1 cm slices • chopped fresh flat-leaf parsley, to garnish • finely chopped fresh mint, to garnish

Preheat the oven to moderately hot 190°C (375°F/Gas 5). Toss all of the vegetables in a large roasting tin with the garlic and 2 tablespoons of the olive oil. Season well. Roast for 40 minutes, or until the vegetables are tender and golden. Whisk the vinegar and the remaining olive oil together until well combined. Arrange the vegetables on a large serving platter and keep warm. Heat a chargrill pan or barbecue plate to very hot, then cook the haloumi for 1–2 minutes on each side, or until dark grill lines appear. Remove and place around the roasted vegetables. Drizzle with the dressing and garnish with the parsley and mint. Serves 4.

GREEK PEPPERED LAMB SALAD

300 g lamb backstraps • 1 1/2 tablespoons black pepper • 3 vine-ripened tomatoes, cut into 8 wedges • 2 Lebanese cucumbers, sliced • 150 g lemon and garlic marinated Kalamata olives, drained (reserving 1 1/2 tablespoons oil) • 100 g Greek feta, cubed • 3/4 teaspoon dried oregano • 1 tablespoon lemon juice • 1 tablespoon extra virgin olive oil

Roll the backstraps in the pepper, pressing the pepper on with your fingers. Cover and refrigerate for 15 minutes. Place the tomato, cucumber, olives, feta and 1/2 teaspoon of the dried oregano in a bowl. Heat a chargrill pan or barbecue plate, brush with oil and when very hot, cook the lamb for 2–3 minutes on each side, or until cooked to your liking. Keep warm. Whisk the lemon juice, extra virgin olive oil, reserved Kalamata oil and the remaining dried oregano together well. Season. Pour half the dressing over the salad, toss together and arrange on a serving platter. Cut the lamb on the diagonal into 1 cm thick slices and arrange on top of the salad. Pour the remaining dressing on top and serve. Serves 4.

CREAMY MUSHROOM SOUP

25 g butter • 1 clove garlic, crushed • 1 small leek, chopped • 2 tablespoons chopped fresh flat-leaf parsley • 3 cups (750 ml) chicken or vegetable stock • 400 g Swiss brown mushrooms, sliced • 200 ml cream • chopped fresh flat-leaf parsley, extra, to garnish

Melt the butter in a large saucepan. Add the garlic, leek and parsley and sauté for 2–3 minutes, or until softened. Pour in the stock and bring to the boil. Reduce the heat and simmer for 3 minutes. Add the mushrooms and simmer for a further 5 minutes. Blend the soup in a food processor in batches until smooth. Return to the cleaned pan, pour in the cream and stir until heated through. Season. Serve, garnished with the extra parsley. Serves 4.

Variation: Stir 300 g thinly sliced chicken breast strips into the stock and cook for 3 minutes before adding the mushrooms.

QUICK MINESTRONE

1 red onion, chopped • 150 g pancetta, finely diced • 2 cloves garlic, crushed • 1 tablespoon tomato paste • 1 litre beef stock • 300 g can cannellini beans, rinsed and drained • 1 cup (250 g) frozen mixed vegetables • 1/3 cup (60 g) tubetti or ditalini pasta • shaved Parmesan, to garnish

Cook the onion and pancetta in a large saucepan over medium heat for 2–3 minutes, or until lightly golden. Add the garlic and cook for 1 minute. Stir in the tomato paste to coat the pancetta mixture. Pour in the stock and bring to the boil. Reduce the heat and add the beans, mixed vegetables and pasta. Simmer for 12–15 minutes, or until the pasta is soft. Serve, garnished with the Parmesan. Serves 4.

Note: For a vegetarian alternative, use vegetable stock instead of beef, and add chickpeas or extra mixed vegetables or pulses rather than pancetta.

ORANGE SWEET POTATO, CAPSICUM AND GINGER SOUP

2 red capsicums, cut into large flat pieces • 1 tablespoon olive oil • 1 small onion, chopped • 2 cloves garlic, chopped • 1 tablespoon grated fresh ginger • 1/4 teaspoon chilli flakes (optional) • 650 g orange sweet potato, cut into 2 cm cubes • 3 cups (750 ml) vegetable stock

Cook the capsicum skin-side-up under a hot grill for 10 minutes, or until the skin blackens and blisters. Cool in a plastic bag, then peel and roughly chop. Heat the olive oil in a large saucepan over medium heat. Add the onion and sauté for 3–4 minutes, or until softened but not coloured. Add the garlic, ginger and chilli flakes and cook for 1 minute. Add the sweet potato and coat well in the onion mixture. Pour in the stock and 1 cup (250 ml) water and simmer for 15–20 minutes, or until the sweet potato is soft. Cool slightly and stir in the capsicum. Blend in a food processor in batches until smooth. Season to taste. Delicious served with a dollop of plain yoghurt. Serves 4.

CHINESE BARBECUE PORK AND NOODLE SOUP

1.25 litres chicken stock • 3 spring onions, cut into 4 cm lengths • 4 thin slices fresh ginger • 1 tablespoon Chinese rice wine • 1 tablespoon oyster sauce • 300 g Chinese barbecue pork fillet, thinly sliced • 2 cups (350 g) roughly chopped bok choy • 200 g fresh flat egg noodles • sliced spring onions, extra, to garnish

Heat the stock and 1 cup (250 ml) water in a large saucepan until simmering. Add the spring onion, ginger, rice wine and oyster sauce and simmer for 3–4 minutes. Add the pork and simmer for a further 4–5 minutes, then add the bok choy. Meanwhile, cook the noodles in a saucepan of salted boiling water for 1 minute. Drain and rinse under cold water, then divide among four deep bowls. When the bok choy has just wilted, remove it and the pork with a slotted spoon, and divide among the serving bowls. Cover with the broth and garnish with the extra spring onion. Serves 4.

PASTA AND RICE

SPAGHETTINI WITH ASPARAGUS AND ROCKET

Preparation time: 15 minutes
Cooking time: 15 minutes
Serves 4

100 ml extra virgin olive oil
16 thin asparagus spears, cut into
    5 cm lengths
375 g spaghettini
120 g rocket, shredded
2 small fresh red chillies, finely
    chopped
2 teaspoons finely grated lemon rind
1 clove garlic, finely chopped
1 cup (100 g) grated Parmesan
2 tablespoons lemon juice

1 Bring a large saucepan of water
to the boil over medium heat. Add
1 tablespoon of the oil and a pinch
of salt to the water and blanch the
asparagus for 3–4 minutes. Remove
the asparagus with a slotted spoon,
refresh under cold water, drain and
place in a bowl. Return the water to
a rapid boil and add the spaghettini.
Cook the pasta according to the
packet instructions until *al dente*.
Drain and return to the pan.

2 Meanwhile, add the rocket, chilli,
lemon rind, garlic and 2/3 cup (65 g)
of the Parmesan to the asparagus
and mix well. Add the mixture to
the cooked pasta, pour on the lemon
juice and the remaining olive oil and
season with salt and freshly ground
black pepper. Stir well to evenly coat
the pasta with the mixture. Divide
among four pasta bowls, top with the
remaining Parmesan and serve.

NUTRITION PER SERVE
Fat 30 g; Protein 21 g; Carbohydrate 66 g;
Dietary Fibre 4.5 g; Cholesterol 20 mg;
2590 kJ (620 Cal)

COOK'S FILE
Variation: This dish is also suitable for
other types of pasta such as tagliatelle,
macaroni or spiral-shaped pasta.

1

2

PASTA WITH PORK AND FENNEL SAUSAGES

Preparation time: 15 minutes
Cooking time: 40 minutes
Serves 4

6 Italian pork and fennel sausages
   (about 550 g)
1 tablespoon olive oil
1 small red onion, finely
   chopped
2–3 cloves garlic, crushed
1/2 teaspoon chilli flakes
300 g field or button mushrooms,
   thinly sliced
2 x 400 g cans diced tomatoes
1 tablespoon finely chopped
   fresh thyme
500 g penne rigate
grated Parmesan, to serve

1 Split the sausages open, remove and crumble the filling, then discard the skins.
2 Heat the oil in a large saucepan over medium–high heat and cook the onion for 3–4 minutes, or until fragrant and transparent. Add the garlic, chilli flakes, mushrooms and crumbled sausage meat. Cook over high heat, stirring gently to mash the sausage meat, for 4–5 minutes, or until the meat is evenly browned. If necessary, use a tablespoon to remove any excess fat from the pan, leaving about a tablespoon of oil. Continue to cook, stirring once or twice, for 10 minutes.

3 Stir in the tomato and thyme, then bring the sauce to the boil. Cover and cook over medium–low heat for 20 minutes, stirring occasionally to make sure the sauce doesn't stick to the bottom of the pan.
4 Meanwhile, cook the pasta in a large saucepan of rapidly boiling salted water according to the packet instructions until *al dente*. Drain well, then add to the sauce, stirring gently to combine. Garnish with Parmesan, then serve immediately with a green salad.

NUTRITION PER SERVE
Fat 36 g; Protein 33.5 g; Carbohydrate 97 g; Dietary Fibre 11.5 g; Cholesterol 73.5 mg; 3555 kJ (850 Cal)

LEMON THYME TUNA WITH TAGLIATELLE

Preparation time: 15 minutes
Cooking time: 15 minutes
Serves 4

375 g tagliatelle
140 ml extra virgin olive oil
1 small fresh red chilli, seeded and finely chopped
1/4 cup (50 g) drained capers
1 1/2 tablespoons fresh lemon thyme leaf tips
500 g tuna steaks, trimmed and cut into 3 cm cubes
1/4 cup (60 ml) lemon juice
1 tablespoon grated lemon rind
1/2 cup (30 g) chopped fresh flat-leaf parsley

1 Cook the pasta in a large saucepan of rapidly boiling salted water according to the packet instructions until *al dente*. Drain, then return to the pan.

2 Meanwhile, heat 1 tablespoon of the oil in a large frying pan. Add the chilli and capers and cook, stirring, for 1 minute, or until the capers are crisp. Add the thyme and cook for 1 more minute. Transfer to a bowl.

3 Heat another tablespoon of oil in the pan. Add the tuna cubes and toss for 2–3 minutes, or until evenly browned on the outside but still pink in the centre—check with the point of a sharp knife. Remove from the heat.

4 Add the tuna to the caper mixture along with the lemon juice, lemon rind, parsley and the remaining oil, stirring gently until combined. Toss through the pasta, season with freshly ground black pepper and serve immediately.

NUTRITION PER SERVE
Fat 39 g; Protein 43 g; Carbohydrate 65.5 g; Dietary Fibre 4 g; Cholesterol 45 mg; 3290 kJ (785 Cal)

CHICKEN AND MUSHROOM PILAU

Preparation time: 15 minutes +
   30 minutes standing
Cooking time: 35 minutes
Serves 4

1¹/2 cups (300 g) basmati rice
2 tablespoons oil
1 large onion, chopped
3–4 cloves garlic, crushed
1 tablespoon finely chopped fresh
   ginger
500 g chicken tenderloin fillets,
   trimmed and cut into small pieces
300 g Swiss brown mushrooms, sliced
3/4 cup (90 g) slivered almonds,
   toasted
1¹/2–2 teaspoons garam masala,
   dry roasted
1/2 cup (125 g) plain yoghurt
1 tablespoon finely chopped fresh
   coriander leaves
fresh coriander leaves, extra,
   to garnish

1 Rinse the rice under cold water until the water runs clear. Drain and leave for 30 minutes. Heat the oil in a large saucepan over medium heat and stir in the onion, garlic and ginger. Cook, covered, for 5 minutes, or until the onion is browned. Increase the heat to high, add the chicken and cook, stirring, for 3–4 minutes, or until the chicken is lightly browned.

2 Stir in the mushrooms, almonds and garam masala. Cook, covered, for another 3 minutes, or until the mushrooms are soft. Remove the lid and cook, stirring, for 2 minutes, or until the liquid evaporates. Remove the chicken pieces from the pan.

3 Add the rice to the pan and stir for 30 seconds, or until well coated in the mushroom and onion mixture. Pour in 1¹/2 cups (375 ml) water and bring to the boil, stirring frequently to prevent the ingredients catching on the bottom of the pan. Cook for 2 minutes, or until most of the water has evaporated. Return the chicken to the pan, reduce the heat to low and steam, covered, for 15 minutes, or until the rice is cooked.

4 Meanwhile, combine the yoghurt and chopped coriander in a small bowl. Fluff the rice with a fork, then divide among serving bowls. Top with a dollop of the yoghurt mixture and garnish with coriander leaves.

NUTRITION PER SERVE
Fat 31.5 g; Protein 38 g; Carbohydrate 67 g; Dietary Fibre 6 g; Cholesterol 112.5 mg; 2933 kJ (698 Cal)

PENNE WITH TOMATO AND ONION JAM WITH OLIVES

Preparation time: 15 minutes
Cooking time: 1 hour
Serves 4

1/4 cup (60 ml) olive oil
4 red onions (650 g), sliced
1 tablespoon soft brown sugar
2 tablespoons balsamic vinegar
2 x 400 g cans tomatoes
500 g penne rigate
150 g small pitted black olives or
    pitted and halved Kalamata olives
3/4 cup (75 g) shaved Parmesan

1 Heat the oil in a non-stick frying pan over medium heat. Add the onion and sugar and cook for 25–30 minutes, or until caramelised.
2 Stir in the vinegar, bring to the boil and cook for 5 minutes. Add the tomatoes, return to the boil, then reduce the heat to medium–low and simmer for 25 minutes, or until the tomatoes are reduced and jam-like.
3 Meanwhile, cook the pasta in a large saucepan of rapidly boiling salted water according to the packet instructions until *al dente*. Drain, then return to the pan. Add the tomato mixture and olives and stir to combine well. Season to taste with salt and black pepper and serve with the Parmesan shavings.

NUTRITION PER SERVE
Fat 20.5 g; Protein 22 g; Carbohydrate 96 g; Dietary Fibre 8.5 g; Cholesterol 15 mg; 2770 kJ (660 Cal)

COOK'S FILE
Notes: Caramelised onions will keep for a few days if covered with oil and stored in the refrigerator.
The onions can be combined with goat's cheese to make a quick puff pastry tart, used as a pizza topping, or to accompany a steak sandwich.

LINGUINE WITH CHARGRILLED BASIL AND LEMON SEAFOOD

Preparation time: 15 minutes +
   10 minutes marinating
Cooking time: 15 minutes
Serves 4

16 raw medium prawns, peeled and
   deveined, with tails intact
350 g calamari rings
1/2 cup (125 ml) extra virgin
   olive oil
1/3 cup (80 ml) lemon juice
3 cloves garlic, crushed
1/2 teaspoon chilli flakes
3 tablespoons chopped fresh basil
400 g linguine
1 teaspoon grated lemon rind

1 Place the prawns and calamari in a non-metallic dish. To make the dressing, combine the olive oil and lemon juice in a small jug, then pour 1/4 cup (60 ml) into a small bowl, reserving the rest. Stir the garlic, chilli flakes and 2 tablespoons of the basil into the bowl, pour over the seafood and mix to coat well. Cover with plastic wrap and marinate in the refrigerator for 5–10 minutes.

2 Cook the pasta in a large saucepan of rapidly boiling salted water according to the packet instructions until *al dente*. Drain, then return to the pan.

3 Meanwhile, preheat a chargrill pan to high and brush with oil. Remove the prawns from the marinade with tongs and cook for 2–3 minutes each side, or until pink and cooked through. Remove. Add the calamari in batches and cook, turning once, for 1–3 minutes, or until opaque and cooked through—take care not to overcrowd the chargrill pan.

4 Transfer the pasta to a large serving bowl, then add the seafood, lemon rind and reserved dressing and gently toss together until the linguine is well coated. Garnish with the remaining basil and season to taste. Serve with a rocket salad.

NUTRITION PER SERVE
Fat 21 g; Protein 36 g; Carbohydrate 69 g; Dietary Fibre 4 g; Cholesterol 245 mg; 2565 kJ (615 Cal)

COOK'S FILE
Note: To save time, use pre-peeled raw prawns from your seafood supplier.
Variation: Toss 1 peeled, seeded and diced tomato through the pasta with the dressing.

ROASTED VEGETABLE CANNELLONI

Preparation time: 15 minutes
Cooking time: 40 minutes
Serves 4

60 g butter
1 large leek, cut into 1 cm pieces
200 g purchased chargrilled eggplant
200 g purchased chargrilled orange
    sweet potato
1 cup (125 g) firmly packed grated
    Cheddar
1/3 cup (40 g) plain flour
1 litre milk
6 fresh lasagne sheets

1 Preheat the oven to moderately hot 200°C (400°F/Gas 6) and lightly grease a large ceramic dish (28 cm x 18 cm x 5 cm). Melt 20 g of the butter in a saucepan, add the leek and cook, stirring, over medium heat for 8 minutes, or until softened. Meanwhile, chop the eggplant and sweet potato into 1 cm pieces and place in a bowl. Mix in the leek and 1/3 cup (40 g) of the Cheddar.

2 Melt the remaining butter in a saucepan over medium heat. Stir in the flour and cook for 1 minute, or until foaming. Remove from the heat and gradually stir in the milk. Return to the heat and stir until the sauce boils and thickens. Reduce the heat and simmer for 2 minutes. Season with salt and freshly ground black pepper. Stir 1 1/2 cups (375 ml) of the sauce into the vegetable mixture, adding a little extra if necessary to bind it all together.

3 Cut the rectangular lasagne sheets in half, down the centre. Spoon some of the vegetable mixture along the centre of one sheet and roll up. Repeat with the remaining pasta sheets and vegetable mixture to make 12 tubes in total.

4 Place the tubes, seam-side-down, in the prepared dish and spoon the remaining white sauce over the top until they are completely covered. Sprinkle with the remaining cheese and bake for about 20 minutes, or until the cheese is golden brown.

NUTRITION PER SERVE
Fat 33.5 g; Protein 23 g; Carbohydrate 51 g; Dietary Fibre 4.5 g; Cholesterol 103.5 mg; 2475 kJ (590 Cal)

COOK'S FILE
Note: Try to buy chargrilled vegetables in oil rather than dressing so it will not change the flavour of the dish. Alternatively, if you have the time, chargrill your own.
Storage: This dish is suitable to freeze.

ORECCHIETTE WITH MUSHROOMS, PANCETTA AND SMOKED MOZZARELLA

Preparation time: 10 minutes
Cooking time: 15 minutes
Serves 4

400 g orecchiette
2 tablespoons olive oil
150 g sliced pancetta, cut into short thin strips
200 g button mushrooms, sliced
2 leeks, sliced
1 cup (250 ml) cream
200 g smoked mozzarella (mozzarella affumicata), cut into 1 cm cubes
8 fresh basil leaves, roughly torn

1 Cook the pasta in a large saucepan of rapidly boiling salted water according to the packet instructions until *al dente*.
2 Meanwhile, heat the oil in a large frying pan and sauté the pancetta, mushrooms and leek over medium–high heat for 5 minutes.

Stir in the cream and season with pepper—the pancetta should provide enough salty flavour. Simmer over low heat for 5 minutes, or until the pasta is ready. Drain the pasta and stir into the frying pan. Add the mozzarella and basil and toss lightly.

NUTRITION PER SERVE
Fat 54 g; Protein 35 g; Carbohydrate 72 g; Dietary Fibre 5.5 g; Cholesterol 140 mg; 3815 kJ (910 Cal)

COOK'S FILE
Note: If you are watching your weight, you can substitute 1/2 cup (125 ml) chicken stock for half of the cream. Smoked provolone can be used instead of the mozzarella, if preferred.

2

PASTA WITH BEEF RAGU

Preparation time: 10 minutes
Cooking time: 1 hour 30 minutes
Serves 4

100 g streaky bacon or pancetta
    (not trimmed), finely chopped
1 onion, finely chopped
3 cloves garlic, crushed
1 bay leaf
800 g lean beef mince
2 cups (500 ml) red wine
1/3 cup (90 g) tomato paste
400 g tagliatelle
freshly grated Parmesan, to garnish

1 Heat a large deep frying pan (preferably stainless steel or non-coated). Add the bacon or pancetta and cook over medium–high heat for 2 minutes, or until soft and just starting to brown. Add the onion, garlic and bay leaf and cook for 2 minutes, or until the onion is soft and just starting to brown.

2 Add the mince and stir for about 4 minutes, or until the mince browns, breaking up any lumps with the back of a wooden spoon. Add the wine, tomato paste and 1 cup (250 ml) water and stir well. Bring to the boil, then reduce the heat and simmer, covered, for 40 minutes. Remove the lid and cook for a further 40 minutes, or until reduced to a thick, glossy sauce.

3 About 20 minutes before the ragù is ready, bring a large saucepan of salted water to a rapid boil and cook the pasta according to the packet instructions until *al dente*. Drain. Serve the sauce over the pasta and garnish with a little grated Parmesan.

NUTRITION PER SERVE
Fat 18.5 g; Protein 58 g; Carbohydrate 72 g; Dietary Fibre 5 g; Cholesterol 116.5 mg; 3250 kJ (775 Cal)

COOK'S FILE
Note: This is a great meal to prepare ahead of time, leaving the flavours to develop overnight. Then all you have to do is reheat it in a saucepan and cook your pasta.

2

3

FRIED RICE WITH CHINESE BARBECUE PORK

Preparation time: 15 minutes
Cooking time: 10 minutes
Serves 4

6 spring onions
150 g snow peas
200 g Chinese barbecue pork
3 teaspoons sesame oil
2 eggs, lightly beaten
2 cloves garlic, finely chopped
3 cups (555 g) cold cooked white
    long-grain rice (see Note)
2 tablespoons soy sauce

1 Cut the spring onions and snow peas diagonally into very thin shreds. Cut the pork into thin slices.
2 Heat a wok until hot, add 1 teaspoon of the oil and swirl to coat the base. Add the egg and swirl over the base until just set. Turn over and cook for 30 seconds, or until just lightly browned, then remove from the wok. Allow the egg to cool slightly, then roll up and cut into 1 cm thick slices.
3 While the wok is still very hot, add the remaining oil, then the garlic, spring onion and snow peas and stir-fry for 1–2 minutes, or until slightly soft. Add the pork, rice, soy sauce and strips of omelette and toss until heated through and thoroughly combined—the soy sauce should turn the rice brown. Remove from the heat and serve immediately.

NUTRITION PER SERVE
Fat 10 g; Protein 22.5 g; Carbohydrate 42 g; Dietary Fibre 2.5 g; Cholesterol 147 mg; 1460 kJ (350 Cal)

COOK'S FILE
Note: Cook 1 cup (200 g) long-grain rice in a large saucepan of boiling water. To cool, spread the rice on a shallow tray and leave uncovered overnight in the refrigerator.

CREAMY GARLIC PRAWN FETTUCCINE

Preparation time: 15 minutes
Cooking time: 20 minutes
Serves 4

400 g fresh fettuccine
2 tomatoes (about 400 g)
1 tablespoon olive oil
1 onion, finely chopped
3 cloves garlic, crushed
1/4 cup (60 ml) white wine
300 ml cream
1 kg raw medium prawns, peeled,
    deveined and tails intact
1/2 cup (15 g) loosely packed roughly
    chopped fresh basil

1 Cook the pasta in a large saucepan of rapidly boiling salted water according to the packet instructions until *al dente*. Drain, then return to the pan.

2 Meanwhile, score a cross in the base of the tomatoes. Place in a heatproof bowl and cover with boiling water. Leave for 30 seconds, then transfer to cold water. Peel the skin away from the cross. Cut in half, scoop out the seeds with a teaspoon and discard. Roughly chop the flesh.

3 Heat the oil in a large frying pan over medium–high heat and cook the onion and garlic, stirring, for 4–5 minutes, or until the onion is soft. Add the tomato and wine and cook for 3 minutes before adding the cream. Bring to the boil, then reduce the heat to medium–low and simmer for 5 minutes, or until it slightly thickens. Stir in the prawns, then simmer for 3–4 minutes, or until the prawns turn pink and are curled and cooked through. Toss with the pasta, gently stir in the basil, season and serve immediately.

NUTRITION PER SERVE
Fat 40 g; Protein 44 g; Carbohydrate 74.5 g; Dietary Fibre 4.5 g; Cholesterol 327 mg; 3530 kJ (845 Cal)

2

3

FREEFORM RICOTTA AND MUSHROOM LASAGNE

Preparation time: 15 minutes
Cooking time: 15 minutes
Serves 4

1 cup (250 g) fresh ricotta
2/3 cup (65 g) grated Parmesan
3 1/2 tablespoons olive oil
1 onion, thinly sliced
2 cloves garlic, crushed
500 g Swiss brown mushrooms, sliced
300 ml good-quality Italian tomato passata
6 sheets fresh lasagne, cut in half, then cut into 12 cm squares
200 g baby English spinach leaves, washed

1 Mix the ricotta with half the Parmesan and season well. Heat 2 tablespoons of the oil in a large frying pan, add the onion and cook for 2 minutes, or until it softens. Add the garlic and mushrooms and continue to cook for 1–2 minutes, or until the mushrooms start to soften. Add the tomato passata and cook for a further 5–6 minutes, or until the sauce starts to thicken. Season well.

2 Meanwhile, bring a deep pan of water to the boil, then add 1 tablespoon of the oil and a pinch of salt. Drop the 12 pasta squares into the boiling water and cook for 2–3 minutes, or until cooked. Drain, keeping each square separate to avoid sticking together. At the same time, put the spinach in a saucepan with just the water clinging to the leaves. Cook, covered, over medium heat for 1–2 minutes, or until the spinach has wilted.

3 To assemble, place one pasta square on each serving plate, then evenly divide the mushroom sauce among the squares. Place another pasta square on top, then spread the ricotta mixture evenly over the surface, leaving a 2 cm border. Divide the spinach evenly among the four servings. Finally, place another pasta square on top, brush or drizzle with the remaining oil, then sprinkle with the remaining Parmesan. Season. Serve with a green salad and crusty bread.

NUTRITION PER SERVE
Fat 25.5 g; Protein 24 g; Carbohydrate 33 g; Dietary Fibre 9.5 g; Cholesterol 44.5 mg; 1920 kJ (460 Cal)

1

2

3

BAKED PRAWN RISOTTO WITH THAI FLAVOURS

Preparation time: 15 minutes
Cooking time: 1 hour
Serves 4

300 ml stock (fish, chicken or
    vegetable)
1 stem lemon grass, bruised
4 fresh kaffir lime leaves, finely
    shredded
2 tablespoons vegetable oil
1 small red onion, thinly sliced
1¹/₂–2 tablespoons good-quality
    Thai red curry paste
1¹/₂ cups (330 g) arborio rice
300 ml coconut cream
600 g raw prawns, peeled and
    deveined with tails intact
    (see Note)

1 Preheat the oven to moderate
180°C (350°F/Gas 4). Pour the stock
into a saucepan, add the lemon grass
and half of the kaffir lime leaves.

Bring to the boil, then reduce the heat
and simmer, covered, for 10 minutes.
2 Heat the oil in a flameproof
casserole dish with a lid. Add the
onion and cook over medium–low
heat for 4–5 minutes, or until soft
but not coloured. Stir in the curry
paste and cook for a further minute,
or until fragrant. Stir in the rice until
well coated. Strain the stock into the
rice then add the coconut cream.
Cover and bake for 15 minutes.
3 Remove from the oven, stir the
risotto well, then bake for a further
10–15 minutes. Add the prawns and
mix them well into the rice—if the
mixture looks a little dry add ¹/₂ cup
(125 ml) stock or water. Bake for a
further 10–15 minutes, or until the
prawns are cooked through and the
rice is tender. Serve the risotto in
bowls garnished with the remaining
shredded lime leaves.

NUTRITION PER SERVE
Fat 29 g; Protein 27 g; Carbohydrate 69.5 g;
Dietary Fibre 3 g; Cholesterol 130.5 mg;
2700 kJ (645 Cal)

COOK'S FILE
Note: To save time, you can purchase
pre-peeled raw prawns with the tails
intact. You will only need 300 g as the
shells make up roughly half the weight
of the prawns.
Variation: You can vary the flavours of
this risotto by using a green curry paste
and/or a variety of seafood (eg. lobster,
calamari, scallops).

2

3

GNOCCHI WITH CREAMY GORGONZOLA AND SAGE SAUCE

Preparation time: 15 minutes
Cooking time: 20 minutes
Serves 4

2 x 500 g packets purchased
    potato gnocchi
60 g butter
2 cloves garlic, crushed
1/2 cup (10 g) fresh small sage leaves
100 g gorgonzola cheese
150 ml cream
1 cup (100 g) grated Parmesan

1 Preheat the grill to high. Lightly grease four 1 cup (250 ml) heatproof gratin dishes. Cook the gnocchi in a large saucepan of rapidly boiling salted water according to the packet instructions until *al dente*. Lift the gnocchi out with a slotted spoon, leave to drain, then divide among the prepared dishes.
2 Melt the butter in a small saucepan over medium heat, add the garlic and sage leaves and cook for a few minutes, or until the leaves start to crispen and the garlic browns a little. Pour the sage butter evenly over the gnocchi in the gratin dishes.
3 Dot small knobs of the gorgonzola evenly among the gnocchi. Pour the cream over the top of each dish and sprinkle with the Parmesan. Place the dishes under the grill and cook until the top starts to brown and the gnocchi are heated through. Serve with a fresh green salad.

NUTRITION PER SERVE
Fat 46 g; Protein 24.5 g; Carbohydrate 75 g; Dietary Fibre 6.5 g; Cholesterol 140.5 mg; 3390 kJ (810 Cal)

COOK'S FILE
Note: This can also be cooked in a 1 litre rectangular heatproof ceramic dish or round pie dish.

MADRAS LAMB PILAU

Preparation time:15 minutes +
  5 minutes marinating
Cooking time: 35 minutes
Serves 4

1/4 cup (60 ml) oil
2 onions, thinly sliced
1 cup (250 g) plain yoghurt
1/4 cup (60 g) good-quality Madras
  curry paste
2 cups (400 g) basmati rice, rinsed
  well
8 large French-trimmed lamb cutlets
4 tablespoons chopped fresh mint
1/2 cup (60 g) slivered almonds,
  lightly toasted

1 Heat 2 tablespoons of the oil in a large saucepan, add the onion and cook over medium heat for 4–5 minutes, or until soft. Remove half with a slotted spoon, set aside and keep warm. Add 200 g of the yoghurt and 2 tablespoons of the curry paste to the pan. Cook, stirring, for 2 minutes. Stir in the rice until well coated. Pour in 2 cups (500 ml) water, bring to the boil, then reduce the heat to medium–low and cook for 15–20 minutes, or until all the water has been absorbed and the rice is tender.

2 Meanwhile, smear the cutlets with the remaining curry paste and marinate for 5 minutes. Heat the remaining oil in a frying pan over high heat, then cook the cutlets for 3–4 minutes on each side, or until cooked to your liking. Remove from the heat, cover with foil and allow to rest. Combine the remaining yoghurt with 1 tablespoon of the mint.

3 To serve, stir the remaining mint through the rice, season, then divide among four serving plates. Top with the remaining onions, the lamb and the almonds. Serve with a dollop of the minted yoghurt on the side.

NUTRITION PER SERVE
Fat 39 g; Protein 46 g; Carbohydrate 87.5 g;
Dietary Fibre 4.5 g; Cholesterol 110 mg;
3720 kJ (890 Cal)

1

2

HAM AND CHEESE PASTA BAKE

Preparation time: 15 minutes
Cooking time: 40 minutes
Serves 4

1½ tablespoons olive oil
1 onion, finely chopped
300 g leg ham, sliced 3 mm thick
    and cut into 5 cm lengths
600 ml light cream

300 g cooked fresh peas or frozen
    peas, thawed
375 g conchiglione (pasta shells)
3 tablespoons roughly chopped
    fresh basil
2 cups (250 g) grated low-fat mature
    Cheddar

1 Preheat the oven to moderately hot 200°C (400°F/Gas 6) and lightly grease a 2.5 litre ovenproof ceramic dish. Heat 1 tablespoon of the oil in a frying pan over medium heat and cook the onion, stirring frequently for 5 minutes, or until soft. Add the remaining oil, then the ham and cook, stirring, for 1 minute. Pour the cream into the pan, bring to the boil, then reduce the heat and simmer for 6 minutes. Add the peas and cook for a further 2–4 minutes, or until the mixture has reduced and thickened slightly. Season with freshly ground black pepper.

2 Meanwhile, cook the pasta in a large saucepan of rapidly boiling salted water according to the packet instructions until *al dente*. Drain, and return to the pan.

3 Add the cream sauce to the pasta, then the basil and three quarters of the cheese. Stir well and season. Transfer the mixture to the prepared dish, sprinkle on the remaining cheese and bake for 20 minutes, or until the top is golden brown.

NUTRITION PER SERVE
Fat 49 g; Protein 53.5 g; Carbohydrate 79 g; Dietary Fibre 7.5 g; Cholesterol 158.5 mg; 4060 kJ (970 Cal)

COOK'S FILE
Ahead of time: Prepare up to 12 hours in advance and keep refrigerated until ready to bake.
Variation: Other pasta shapes such as spirals, farfalle, fusilli or macaroni are suitable for this dish.

SPANISH SAFFRON CHICKEN AND RICE

Preparation time: 10 minutes
Cooking time: 1 hour
Serves 4

1/4 cup (60 ml) olive oil
4 chicken thighs and 6 drumsticks
1 large red onion, finely chopped
1 large green capsicum, two thirds
    diced and one third julienned
3 teaspoons sweet paprika
400 g can diced tomatoes
1 1/4 cups (275 g) paella or arborio
    rice (see Note)
1/2 teaspoon ground saffron

1 Heat 2 tablespoons of the oil in a large deep frying pan over high heat. Season the chicken pieces well and brown in batches. Remove the chicken from the pan.
2 Reduce the pan to medium heat and add the remaining oil. Add the onion and the diced capsicum and cook gently for 5 minutes. Stir in the paprika and cook for 30 seconds. Add the tomato and simmer for 1–3 minutes, or until it thickens.
3 Stir in 3 1/2 cups (875 ml) boiling water to the pan, then add the rice and saffron. Return the chicken to the pan and stir to combine. Season to taste. Bring to the boil, then cover, reduce the heat to medium–low and simmer for 20–30 minutes, or until all the liquid has been absorbed and the chicken is tender. Stir in the julienned capsicum, then allow to stand, covered, for 3–4 minutes before serving.

NUTRITION PER SERVE
Fat 44.5 g; Protein 92 g; Carbohydrate 57 g; Dietary Fibre 2.5 g; Cholesterol 432.5 mg; 4150 kJ (990 Cal)

COOK'S FILE
Note: Paella rice is a medium round grain from Spain. Calasparra is the most commonly available variety and can be purchased from fine food stores or Spanish delicatessens.

GRILLS AND BARBECUES

ROSEMARY AND RED WINE STEAKS WITH BARBECUED VEGETABLES

Preparation time: 15 minutes +
   25 minutes marinating
Cooking time: 45 minutes
Serves 4

12 small new potatoes
1/4 cup (60 ml) olive oil
1 tablespoon finely chopped fresh
   rosemary
6 cloves garlic, sliced
sea salt flakes, to season
4 large, thick field mushrooms
12 asparagus spears
1 cup (250 ml) red wine
4 scotch fillet steaks (about 260 g
   each)

1 Heat a barbecue plate or chargrill pan to hot. Toss the potatoes with 1 tablespoon of the oil, half the rosemary and half the garlic and season with the sea salt flakes. Divide the potatoes among four large sheets of foil (three potatoes per sheet) and wrap up into neat packages, sealing firmly around the edges. Place on the barbecue and cook, turning frequently for about 30–40 minutes, or until tender.

2 Meanwhile, brush the mushrooms and asparagus with a little of the remaining oil and set aside.

3 Combine the red wine with the remaining oil, rosemary and garlic in a non-metallic dish. Season with lots of freshly ground black pepper. Add the steaks and turn to coat well in the marinade. Allow to marinate for 25 minutes, then drain.

4 Place the steaks on the barbecue with the mushrooms and cook for 4 minutes each side, or until cooked to your liking (this will depend on the thickness of your steak). Transfer the steaks and mushrooms to a plate, cover lightly and allow to rest. Add the asparagus to the barbecue, turning regularly for about 2 minutes, or until tender. By this stage your potatoes should be cooked—open the foil and pierce with a skewer to check for doneness. Season with salt and pepper. Serve a steak per person, accompanied by a mushroom, three asparagus spears and a potato package.

NUTRITION PER SERVE
Fat 25.5 g; Protein 61 g; Carbohydrate 25 g;
Dietary Fibre 5.5 g; Cholesterol 174 mg;
2600 kJ (620 Cal)

1

4

SUMAC-CRUSTED LAMB FILLETS WITH BABA GANOUJ

Preparation time: 15 minutes
Cooking time: 25 minutes
Serves 4

2 tablespoons olive oil
750 g small new potatoes
2–3 cloves garlic, crushed
1/4 cup (60 ml) lemon juice
1 red capsicum, seeded and
    quartered lengthways
4 lamb backstraps (about 200 g each)
1 tablespoon sumac (see Note)
3 tablespoons finely chopped fresh
    flat-leaf parsley
250 g good-quality baba ganouj
    (eggplant dip)

1 Heat the oil in a saucepan big enough to hold the potatoes in one layer. Add the potatoes and garlic, and cook, turning frequently, for 3–5 minutes, or until brown all over. When golden, add the lemon juice and reduce the heat to medium–low. Gently simmer, covered, for 15–20 minutes, or until tender; stir occasionally to prevent sticking. Remove from the heat. Season well.

2 Meanwhile, lightly oil a chargrill pan or barbecue plate and heat to very hot. Cook the capsicum pieces skin-side-down for 1–2 minutes, or until the skin starts to blister and turn black. Cook the other side for 1–2 minutes. Remove from the heat, then place in a plastic bag or bowl covered with plastic wrap. Set aside.
3 Coat the lamb with sumac. Cook on the chargrill pan for 4–5 minutes on each side, or until cooked to your liking. Remove from the heat, cover with foil and rest. Remove the skin from the capsicum and slice the quarters into thin strips.
4 Stir the parsley through the potatoes. Divide the baba ganouj among four plates. Cut the lamb into 1 cm slices on the diagonal and arrange on top of the baba ganouj with the capsicum strips. Serve with the potatoes and a green salad.

NUTRITION PER SERVE
Fat 18 g; Protein 47 g; Carbohydrate 29 g; Dietary Fibre 6 g; Cholesterol 130.5 mg; 1965 kJ (470 Cal)

COOK'S FILE
Note: Sumac is available from Middle Eastern grocery stores and some gourmet food retailers. If unavailable, use the same amount of ground cumin.

1

2

BARBECUED CHERMOULA PRAWNS

Preparation time: 15 minutes +
  10 minutes standing
Cooking time: 10 minutes
Serves 4

1 kg raw medium prawns
3 teaspoons hot paprika
2 teaspoons ground cumin
1 cup (30 g) firmly packed fresh
  flat-leaf parsley
1/2 cup (15 g) firmly packed fresh
  coriander leaves
100 ml lemon juice
145 ml olive oil
11/2 cups (280 g) couscous
1 tablespoon grated lemon rind
lemon wedges, to serve

1 Peel the prawns, leaving the tails intact. Gently pull out the dark vein from the backs, starting at the head end. Place the prawns in a large bowl. Dry-fry the paprika and cumin in a frying pan for about 1 minute, or until fragrant. Remove from the heat.
2 Blend or process the spices, parsley, coriander, lemon juice and 1/2 cup (125 ml) of the oil until finely chopped. Add a little salt and pepper. Pour over the prawns and mix well, then cover with plastic wrap and refrigerate for 10 minutes. Heat a chargrill pan or barbecue plate to hot.
3 Meanwhile, to cook the couscous, bring 1 cup (250 ml) water to the boil in a saucepan, then stir in the couscous, lemon rind, the remaining oil and 1/4 teaspoon salt. Remove

from the heat, cover and leave for 5 minutes. Fluff the couscous with a fork, adding a little extra olive oil if needed.
4 Cook the prawns on the chargrill pan for about 3–4 minutes, or until cooked through, turning and brushing with extra marinade while cooking (take care not to overcook). Serve the prawns on a bed of couscous, with a wedge of lemon.

NUTRITION PER SERVE
Fat 31 g; Protein 35.5 g; Carbohydrate 56 g; Dietary Fibre 1.5 g; Cholesterol 186 mg; 2705 kJ (645 Cal)

1

TANDOORI CHICKEN WITH CARDAMOM RICE

Preparation time: 15 minutes +
    30 minutes soaking +
    10 minutes marinating
Cooking time: 25 minutes
Serves 4

200 g plain yoghurt, plus extra
    for serving
1/4 cup (60 g) good-quality tandoori
    paste
2 tablespoons lemon juice
1 kg chicken breast fillets,
    cut into 3 cm cubes
1 tablespoon oil
1 onion, finely diced
1 1/2 cups (300 g) long-grain rice
2 cardamom pods, bruised
3 cups (750 ml) hot chicken stock
400 g English spinach leaves

1 Soak eight wooden skewers in water for 30 minutes to prevent them burning during cooking. Combine the yoghurt, tandoori paste and lemon juice in a non-metallic dish. Add the chicken and coat well, then cover and marinate for at least 10 minutes.

2 Meanwhile, heat the oil in a saucepan. Add the onion and cook for 3 minutes, then add the rice and cardamom pods. Cook, stirring often, for 3–5 minutes, or until the rice is slightly opaque. Add the stock and bring to the boil. Reduce the heat to low, cover, and cook, without removing the lid, for 15 minutes.

3 Heat a barbecue plate or oven grill to very hot. Thread the chicken cubes onto the skewers, leaving the bottom quarter of the skewers empty. Cook on each side for 4–5 minutes, or until cooked through.

4 Wash the spinach and place in a large saucepan with just the water clinging to the leaves. Cook, covered, over medium heat for 1–2 minutes, or until the spinach has wilted. Uncover the rice, fluff with a fork and serve with the spinach, chicken and extra yoghurt.

NUTRITION PER SERVE
Fat 25.5 g; Protein 67 g; Carbohydrate 67 g; Dietary Fibre 5 g; Cholesterol 171 mg; 3230 kJ (770 Cal)

COOK'S FILE

Ahead of time: Marinate the chicken for up to 48 hours in advance.

BARBECUED ASIAN PORK RIBS WITH SPRING ONION RICE

Preparation time: 15 minutes +
  10 minutes marinating
Cooking time: 40 minutes
Serves 4

1 kg American-style pork ribs,
  cut into sections of 4–5 ribs
$1/4$ cup (60 ml) hoisin sauce
1 tablespoon Chinese rice wine
  or dry sherry
$1/4$ cup (60 ml) soy sauce
2 cloves garlic, chopped
2 tablespoons oil
3 spring onions, finely chopped
1 tablespoon grated fresh ginger
$1^1/4$ cups (250 g) jasmine rice
600 g baby bok choy, leaves
  separated

1 Place the ribs in a non-metallic bowl. Combine the hoisin sauce, rice wine, soy sauce, garlic, 1 tablespoon of the oil, 2 tablespoons of the spring onion and half the ginger. Pour onto the ribs and mix to coat. Marinate for at least 10 minutes, or overnight in the refrigerator.

2 Bring a large saucepan of water to the boil. Add the rice and cook for 12 minutes, stirring occasionally. Drain well.

3 Heat the remaining oil in a small saucepan over medium–low heat. When the oil is warm but not smoking, remove the pan from the heat and add the remaining spring onion and ginger. Season with $1/4$ teaspoon salt, stirring quickly to combine. Stir this mixture through the rice.

4 Preheat a chargrill pan or barbecue plate and brush with oil. Remove the ribs from the marinade with tongs and reserve the marinade. Cook the ribs in batches, if necessary, for 8–10 minutes on each side, or until cooked through, basting with the marinade during cooking.

5 Five minutes before the ribs are cooked, place the reserved marinade in a saucepan and bring to the boil (add $1/3$ cup/80 ml water if there is not much liquid). Boil for 2 minutes, then add the bok choy, stirring to coat. Cook, covered, for 1–2 minutes, or until just wilted. Serve the ribs with the rice and bok choy, and drizzle with the marinade.

NUTRITION PER SERVE
Fat 25.5 g; Protein 43 g; Carbohydrate 59 g; Dietary Fibre 4.5 g; Cholesterol 113.5 mg; 2690 kJ (640 Cal)

3

4

PAPRIKA LAMB KEBABS WITH SKORDALIA

Preparation time: 15 minutes +
    30 minutes soaking
Cooking time: 30 minutes
Serves 4

1 kg lamb backstraps, cut into
    2 cm cubes
1 tablespoon sweet paprika
1 tablespoon hot paprika
1/2 cup (125 ml) lemon juice
1/2 cup (125 ml) olive oil
3 large (750 g) floury potatoes
    (e.g. russet), cut into large cubes
3–4 cloves garlic, crushed with a
    pinch of salt
300 g English spinach leaves
lemon wedges, to serve

1 Soak 12 wooden skewers in water for 30 minutes to prevent them burning during cooking. Thread six lamb cubes onto each skewer, then place in a non-metallic rectangular dish large enough to hold all of the skewers in one layer.

2 To make the marinade, combine both the paprikas, 1/3 cup (80 ml) of the lemon juice and 1/4 cup (60 ml) of the oil in a small non-metallic jug. Pour over the skewers, turning to ensure they are well coated. Season with pepper. Cover and refrigerate while making the skordalia.

3 To make the skordalia, boil the potatoes for 20 minutes, or until tender. Drain and place the potatoes, garlic and 1 tablespoon of the lemon juice in a food processor. With the motor running, slowly add the remaining oil in a thin stream and continue blending for 30–60 seconds, or until all the oil is incorporated— avoid overprocessing as it will become gluey. Season. Set aside to serve at room temperature.

4 Preheat a chargrill pan or barbecue plate and brush with oil. Add the skewers and chargrill for 3–4 minutes on each side for medium–rare, or 5–6 minutes for well done.

5 Meanwhile, wash the spinach and add to a saucepan with just the water clinging to the leaves. Cook, covered, over medium heat for 1–2 minutes, or until the spinach has wilted. Remove from the heat and stir in the remaining lemon juice. Serve the kebabs immediately with the skordalia, spinach and lemon wedges.

NUTRITION PER SERVE
Fat 35.5 g; Protein 58 g; Carbohydrate 27 g; Dietary Fibre 6 g; Cholesterol 162.5 mg; 2780 kJ (665 Cal)

COOK'S FILE
Variation: Alternate cherry tomatoes, onion wedges or pieces of capsicum and zucchini with the lamb cubes.

CAJUN CHICKEN WITH FRESH TOMATO AND CORN SALSA

Preparation time: 15 minutes
Cooking time: 15 minutes
Serves 4

2 corn cobs
2 vine-ripened tomatoes, diced
1 Lebanese cucumber, diced
2 tablespoons roughly chopped
    fresh coriander leaves
4 chicken breast fillets
    (about 200 g each)
1/4 cup (35 g) Cajun seasoning
2 tablespoons lime juice
lime wedges, to serve

1 Cook the corn cobs in a saucepan of boiling water for 5 minutes, or until tender. Remove the kernels using a sharp knife and place in a bowl with the tomato, cucumber and coriander. Season and mix well.

2 Heat a chargrill pan or barbecue plate to medium heat and brush lightly with oil. Pound each chicken breast between two sheets of plastic wrap with a mallet or rolling pin until 2 cm thick. Lightly coat the chicken with the Cajun seasoning and shake off any excess. Cook for 5 minutes on each side, or until just cooked through.

3 Just before serving, stir the lime juice into the salsa. Place a chicken breast on each serving plate and spoon the salsa on the side. Serve with the lime wedges, a green salad and crusty bread.

NUTRITION PER SERVE
Fat 7 g; Protein 26 g; Carbohydrate 16.5 g; Dietary Fibre 5 g; Cholesterol 66 mg; 980 kJ (235 Cal)

1

2

VEGETABLE SKEWERS WITH BASIL COUSCOUS

Preparation time: 15 minutes +
   30 minutes soaking +
   10 minutes standing
Cooking time: 15 minutes
Serves 4

5 thin zucchini, cut into 2 cm cubes
5 slender eggplants, cut into 2 cm
   cubes
12 button mushrooms, halved
2 red capsicums, cut into 1.5 cm
   cubes
250 g kefalotyri cheese, cut into
   2 cm thick pieces (see Note)
1/3 cup (80 ml) lemon juice
2 garlic cloves, finely chopped
5 tablespoons finely chopped
   fresh basil
145 ml extra virgin olive oil
1 cup (185 g) couscous
1 teaspoon grated lemon rind

1 Soak 12 wooden skewers in water for 30 minutes to prevent them burning during cooking. Thread alternate pieces of vegetables and kefalotyri, starting and finishing with a piece of capsicum and using two pieces of kefalotyri per skewer. Place in a non-metallic dish large enough to hold them in one layer.
2 Combine the lemon juice, garlic, 4 tablespoons of the basil and 1/2 cup (125 ml) of the oil in a non-metallic bowl. Season. Pour two thirds of the marinade over the skewers, reserving the remainder. Turn the skewers to coat evenly, cover with plastic wrap and marinate for at least 5 minutes.
3 Place the couscous, lemon rind and 1 1/2 cups (375 ml) boiling water in a large heatproof bowl. Stand for 5 minutes, or until all the water has been absorbed. Add the remaining oil and basil, then fluff gently with a fork to separate the grains. Cover.
4 Meanwhile, heat a chargrill pan or barbecue plate to medium–high. Cook the skewers, brushing often with the leftover marinade in the non-metallic dish, for 4–5 minutes on each side, or until the vegetables are cooked and the cheese browns—take care that the cheese doesn't fall apart during cooking.
5 Divide the couscous and skewers among four serving plates. Season, then drizzle with the reserved marinade to taste. Serve immediately with lemon wedges, if desired.

NUTRITION PER SERVE
Fat 50.5 g; Protein 24 g; Carbohydrate 41 g; Dietary Fibre 4 g; Cholesterol 56 mg; 2965 kJ (710 Cal)

COOK'S FILE
Note: Kefalotyri can be found in continental delicatessens and in some larger supermarkets. If not available, use haloumi instead.

LIME AND CORIANDER CHARGRILLED CHICKEN

Preparation time: 15 minutes +
   1 hour marinating
Cooking time: 15 minutes
Serves 4

3 teaspoons finely grated fresh ginger
1/2 cup (25 g) chopped fresh
   coriander leaves
11/2 teaspoons grated lime rind
1/3 cup (80 ml) lime juice
4 skinless chicken breast fillets
   (about 750 g), trimmed
11/4 cups (250 g) jasmine rice
2 tablespoons oil
3 zucchini, cut into wedges
4 large flat mushrooms, stalks
   trimmed

1 Combine the ginger, coriander, lime rind and 2 tablespoons of the lime juice. Spread 2 teaspoons of the herb mixture over each fillet and season well. Marinate for 1 hour. Combine the remaining herb mixture with the remaining lime juice in a screwtop jar. Set aside until needed.
2 Bring a large saucepan of water to the boil. Add the rice and cook for 12 minutes, stirring occasionally. Drain well.
3 Meanwhile, heat a chargrill pan or barbecue plate to medium and lightly brush with oil. Brush the zucchini and mushrooms with the remaining oil. Place the chicken on the chargrill and cook on each side for 4–5 minutes, or until cooked through. Add the vegetables during the last 5 minutes of cooking, and turn frequently until browned on the outside and just softened. Cover with foil until ready to serve.
4 Divide the rice among four serving bowls. Cut the chicken fillets into long thick strips, then arrange on top of the rice. Shake the dressing well and drizzle over the chicken and serve with the chargrilled vegetables.

NUTRITION PER SERVE
Fat 20.5 g; Protein 47 g; Carbohydrate 52 g; Dietary Fibre 3 g; Cholesterol 123.5 mg; 2435 kJ (580 Cal)

COOK'S FILE
Note: Allow 5 minutes for the chargrill pan to heat evenly to medium heat. Do not cook on a smoking hot grill or the chicken will singe, overcooking the outside and not evenly throughout.

1

4

LAMB CUTLETS WITH MINT GREMOLATA

Preparation time: 15 minutes
Cooking time: 10 minutes
Serves 4

4 tablespoons fresh mint leaves
1 tablespoon fresh flat-leaf parsley
2 cloves garlic
1¹/₂ tablespoons lemon rind (white pith removed), cut into thin strips
2 tablespoons extra virgin olive oil
8 French-trimmed lamb cutlets
2 carrots
2 zucchini
1 tablespoon lemon juice

1 To make the gremolata, finely chop the mint, parsley, garlic and lemon strips, then combine well.
2 Heat a chargrill pan or barbecue plate to very hot. Lightly brush with 1 tablespoon of the oil. Cook the cutlets over medium heat for 2 minutes on each side, or until cooked to your liking. Remove the cutlets and cover to keep warm.
3 Trim the ends from the carrots and zucchini and, using a sharp vegetable peeler, peel the vegetables lengthways into ribbons. Heat the remaining oil in a large saucepan, add the vegetables and toss over medium heat for 3–5 minutes, or until sautéed but tender.
4 Divide the cutlets among the serving plates, sprinkle the cutlets with the gremolata and drizzle with the lemon juice. Serve with the vegetable ribbons.

NUTRITION PER SERVE
Fat 19 g; Protein 40 g; Carbohydrate 3 g; Dietary Fibre 2.5 g; Cholesterol 130 mg; 1445 kJ (345 Cal)

COOK'S FILE
Hint: Use a vegetable peeler to remove the rind from the lemon.

BARBECUED STEAK WITH CARAMELISED BALSAMIC ONIONS AND MUSTARD CREME FRAICHE

Preparation time: 15 minutes
Cooking time: 35 minutes
Serves 4

1¹/₂ tablespoons wholegrain mustard
200 g crème fraîche
2 capsicums (1 red and 1 yellow), seeded and quartered
2 zucchini, trimmed and sliced lengthways into strips
2 tablespoons oil
2 large red onions, thinly sliced
4 rump steaks (about 200 g each)
2 tablespoons soft brown sugar
¹/₄ cup (60 ml) balsamic vinegar

1 Preheat a flat barbecue hotplate or large chargrill pan to hot. Combine the mustard and crème fraîche in a bowl. Season. Cover and set aside.
2 Brush the capsicum and zucchini with 1 tablespoon of the oil. Cook the capsicum, turning regularly, on the hotplate for 5 minutes, or until tender and slightly charred. Remove and cover with foil. Repeat with the zucchini, also cooking for 5 minutes.
3 Heat the remaining oil on the hotplate, then cook the onion, turning occasionally, for 5–10 minutes, or until softened. When nearly soft, push to the side of the hotplate, then add the steaks and cook on each side for 3–4 minutes (medium-rare), or until cooked to your liking. Remove the steaks, cover with foil and allow to rest. Spread the onion over the hotplate once again, reduce the heat, sprinkle with sugar and cook for 1–2 minutes, or until the sugar has dissolved and the onion appear glossy. Add the vinegar, stirring continuously for 1–2 minutes, or until it is absorbed. Remove at once.
4 Peel the skin off the capsicum, then divide among four serving plates with the zucchini. Place the steaks on top, season and top with the balsamic onions. Serve with the mustard crème fraîche and a mixed leaf salad.

NUTRITION PER SERVE
Fat 35 g; Protein 50 g; Carbohydrate 13 g; Dietary Fibre 2 g; Cholesterol 175.5 mg; 2365 kJ (565 Cal)

3

PAN-FRIES AND STIR-FRIES

STUFFED CHICKEN BREAST WITH TOMATO, GOAT'S CHEESE AND ASPARAGUS

Preparation time: 15 minutes
Cooking time: 20 minutes
Serves 4

4 large chicken breast fillets
100 g semi-dried tomatoes
100 g mild goat's cheese, sliced
200 g asparagus spears, trimmed, halved and blanched
50 g butter
1½ cups (375 ml) chicken stock
2 zucchini, cut into 5 cm batons
1 cup (250 ml) cream
8 spring onions, thinly sliced

1 Pound each chicken breast between two sheets of plastic wrap with a mallet or rolling pin until 1 cm thick. Divide the tomato, goat's cheese and 155 g of the asparagus pieces among the breasts. Roll up tightly lengthways, securing along the seam with toothpicks.

2 Heat the butter in a large frying pan over medium heat. Add the chicken, then brown on all sides. Pour in the stock, then reduce the heat to low. Cook, covered, for 10 minutes, or until the chicken is cooked through. Remove the chicken and keep warm.

3 Meanwhile, bring a saucepan of lightly salted water to the boil. Add the zucchini and remaining asparagus and cook for 2 minutes, or until just tender. Remove from the pan.

4 Whisk the cream into the frying pan. Add the spring onion and simmer over medium–low heat for 4 minutes, or until reduced and thickened.

5 To serve, cut each chicken roll in half on the diagonal and place on serving plates. Spoon on the sauce and serve with the greens.

NUTRITION PER SERVE
Fat 63.5 g; Protein 90 g; Carbohydrate 10 g; Dietary Fibre 4 g; Cholesterol 377 mg; 4045 kJ (965 Cal)

1

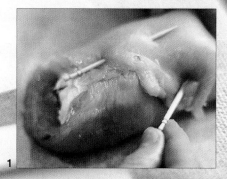

1

FILLET STEAK WITH MIXED MUSHROOMS AND SHERRY

Preparation time: 10 minutes
Cooking time: 20 minutes
Serves 4

250 g broccoli, cut into large florets
250 g green beans, top and tailed
1 tablespoon oil
60 g butter
4 rib eye steaks (scotch fillet)
    (about 160 g each), 2.5 cm thick
3 cloves garlic, finely chopped
250 g mixed mushrooms (portabella,
    Swiss brown, shiitake or button)
2 teaspoons chopped fresh thyme
1/2 cup (125 ml) dry sherry

1 Bring a saucepan of lightly salted water to the boil. Add the broccoli and beans and cook for 3–4 minutes, or until tender but still crisp. Drain.
2 Melt the oil and 20 g of the butter in a large stainless steel frying pan. Cook the steaks for 3–4 minutes on each side for medium–rare, or until cooked to your liking. Remove from the pan, cover with foil and rest.
3 Melt another 20 g of the butter in the pan over medium heat. Add the garlic and mushrooms and season to taste. Cook for 3–4 minutes, or until the mushrooms have softened. Stir in the thyme. Remove from the pan.
4 Add the sherry and any juices from the rested meat to the pan and stir well to scrape up any sediment stuck to the base. Bring to the boil,

then reduce the heat and simmer for 2–3 minutes, or until reduced to 1/3 cup (80 ml) and thickened slightly. Whisk in the remaining butter in small amounts, until glossy.
5 To serve, put the steaks on four serving plates, top with the mushrooms and spoon the sauce over the top. Serve with the broccoli and green beans.

NUTRITION PER SERVE
Fat 25 g; Protein 40.5 g; Carbohydrate 3.5 g; Dietary Fibre 6.5 g; Cholesterol 145.5 mg; 1810 kJ (435 Cal)

COOK'S FILE
Note: Exotic mushrooms are available pre-packaged in most supermarkets.
Variation: Use red wine instead of sherry, or parsley instead of thyme.

4

4

SWORDFISH WITH TOMATO SALSA AND GARLIC MASH

Preparation time: 15 minutes
Cooking time: 25 minutes
Serves 4

500 g potatoes, cubed
2 large vine-ripened tomatoes
2 tablespoons finely shredded
    fresh basil
1 tablespoon balsamic vinegar
3 cloves garlic, finely chopped
145 ml olive oil
4 swordfish steaks (about 200 g each)

1 Cook the potato in a large saucepan of boiling water for 12–15 minutes, or until tender.

2 To make the salsa, score a cross in the base of each tomato. Place in a heatproof bowl and cover with boiling water. Leave for 30 seconds, then plunge into iced water and peel the skin away from the cross. Cut the tomatoes in half, scoop out the seeds with a teaspoon and discard. Finely dice the flesh, then combine with the basil, vinegar, 2 cloves of the garlic and 2 tablespoons of the oil. Season.

3 Heat $1/4$ cup (60 ml) of the olive oil in a large non-stick frying pan over medium–high heat. Season the swordfish well, then add to the frying pan and cook for 2–3 minutes on each side for medium–rare, or until cooked to your liking.

4 Just before the swordfish is ready, drain the potato. Add the remaining olive oil and garlic, and season to taste. Mash until smooth with a potato masher.

5 To serve, put the swordfish steaks on four serving plates and top with the tomato salsa. Serve the garlic mash on the side.

NUTRITION PER SERVE
Fat 36.5 g; Protein 43 g; Carbohydrate 19 g; Dietary Fibre 3.5 g; Cholesterol 112 mg; 2395 kJ (570 Cal)

2

TOFU, SNOW PEA AND MUSHROOM STIR-FRY

Preparation time: 10 minutes
Cooking time: 15 minutes
Serves 4

1¼ cups (250 g) jasmine rice
¼ cup (60 ml) peanut oil
600 g firm tofu, drained, cut into
    2 cm cubes
2 teaspoons sambal oelek or chilli
    paste
2 cloves garlic, finely chopped
400 g fresh Asian mushrooms, sliced
    (shiitake, oyster or black fungus)
300 g snow peas, trimmed
¼ cup (60 ml) kecap manis

1 Bring a large saucepan of water to the boil. Add the rice and cook for 12 minutes, stirring occasionally. Drain well.
2 Meanwhile, heat a wok until very hot. Add 2 tablespoons of the oil and swirl to coat. Stir-fry the tofu in two batches on all sides for 2–3 minutes, or until lightly browned, then transfer to a plate.
3 Add the remaining oil to the wok, add the sambal oelek, garlic, mushrooms, snow peas and 1 tablespoon water and stir-fry for 1–2 minutes, or until the vegetables are almost cooked but still crunchy.
4 Return the tofu to the wok, add the kecap manis and stir-fry for another minute, or until heated through and combined. Serve immediately with the rice.

NUTRITION PER SERVE
Fat 23.5 g; Protein 29 g; Carbohydrate 57 g; Dietary Fibre 10 g; Cholesterol 0 mg; 2315 kJ (555 Cal)

COOK'S FILE
Note: Firm tofu is suitable to stir-fry as it will hold its shape.
Variation: Use 3 teaspoons grated fresh ginger instead of the sambal oelek.

2

3

SATAY CHICKEN STIR-FRY

Preparation time: 10 minutes
Cooking time: 20 minutes
Serves 4

1¹/2 cups (250 g) jasmine rice
1¹/2 tablespoons peanut oil
6 spring onions, cut into 3 cm lengths
800 g chicken breast fillets, thinly
    sliced on the diagonal
1–1¹/2 tablespoons good-quality
    Thai red curry paste
¹/3 cup (90 g) crunchy peanut butter
270 ml coconut milk
2 teaspoons soft brown sugar
1¹/2 tablespoons lime juice

1 Bring a large saucepan of water to the boil. Add the rice and cook for 12 minutes, stirring occasionally. Drain well.

2 Meanwhile, heat a wok until very hot, add 1 teaspoon of the peanut oil and swirl to coat. When hot, add the spring onion and stir-fry for 30 seconds, or until softened slightly. Remove from the wok. Add a little extra peanut oil to the wok as needed and stir-fry the chicken in three batches for about 1 minute per batch, or until the meat just changes colour. Remove from the wok.

3 Add a little more oil to the wok, add the curry paste and stir-fry for 1 minute, or until fragrant. Add the peanut butter, coconut milk, sugar and 1 cup (250 ml) water and stir well. Bring to the boil and boil for 3–4 minutes, or until thickened and the oil starts to separate—reduce the heat slightly if the sauce spits at you. Return the chicken and the spring onion to the wok, stir well and cook for 2 minutes, or until heated through. Stir in the lime juice and season. Serve at once with the rice and a crisp green salad.

NUTRITION PER SERVE
Fat 46 g; Protein 55 g; Carbohydrate 57.5 g;
Dietary Fibre 5.5 g; Cholesterol 132 mg;
3600 kJ (860 Cal)

LAMB BACKSTRAPS WITH SPICED LENTILS AND MINT RAITA

Preparation time: 15 minutes +
  10 minutes marinating
Cooking time: 20 minutes
Serves 4

1/2 cup (125 g) plain yoghurt
2 tablespoons finely chopped
  fresh mint
1 tablespoon garam masala
3 teaspoons ground cumin
1/2 teaspoon chilli powder
1/3 cup (80 ml) oil
4 lamb backstraps (about 150 g each)
2 teaspoons grated fresh ginger
1 teaspoon ground turmeric
2 x 425 g cans lentils, drained and
  rinsed

1 Combine the yoghurt and half the mint in a small non-metallic bowl. Cover and set aside.
2 Place the garam masala in a small dry frying pan and dry-fry over medium heat for 1 minute, or until fragrant. Remove from the pan, then repeat with the ground cumin. Combine the chilli, 2 teaspoons of the garam masala, 2 teaspoons of the cumin and 2 tablespoons of the oil. Place the lamb in a non-metallic dish and brush with the spiced oil. Cover and marinate for at least 10 minutes, or overnight, if time permits.
3 Meanwhile, heat 1 tablespoon of the remaining oil in a saucepan. Add the ginger, turmeric and remaining cumin and cook for 30 seconds, or until fragrant. Add the lentils and stir thoroughly until heated through. Reduce the heat to low, add the remaining garam masala and season well with salt. Cook, covered, for 5 minutes, adding 1/4 cup (60 ml) water if the lentils start to stick. Before serving, stir in the remaining mint.
4 Heat a large frying pan over medium–high heat and add the remaining oil. Add the backstraps and cook for 3–4 minutes each side for medium–rare, or until cooked to your liking. Allow to rest for several minutes, then cut into 1 cm slices on the diagonal.
5 To serve, place a small mound of lentils on a plate, arrange the lamb slices on top and serve with a dollop of mint raita. Garnish with fresh mint, if desired.

NUTRITION PER SERVE
Fat 24.5 g; Protein 40 g; Carbohydrate 15 g; Dietary Fibre 5 g; Cholesterol 101.5 mg; 1840 kJ (440 Cal)

2

4

BEEF STROGANOFF

Preparation time: 15 minutes
Cooking time: 20 minutes
Serves 4

600 g rib eye fillet or rump
1/4 cup (30 g) seasoned plain flour
375 g fettuccine or tagliatelle
60 g butter
1 small onion, finely chopped
300 g button mushrooms, thickly sliced
1 tablespoon tomato paste
1/4 cup (60 ml) red wine
300 ml cream

1 Pound the slices of beef between two sheets of plastic wrap with a mallet or rolling pin until half their thickness. Cut each slice into strips about 1 cm wide. Place in a plastic bag with the seasoned flour and shake to coat.

2 Bring a large saucepan of water to the boil and cook the fettuccine according to the packet instructions, until *al dente*.

3 Meanwhile, melt 40 g of the butter in a frying pan over medium heat and cook the onion for 2 minutes. Add the beef in batches and cook for 5 minutes, or until evenly browned. Remove from the pan and keep warm. Heat the remaining butter in the pan and add the mushrooms, stirring, for 2–3 minutes, or until soft and lightly browned. Add the tomato paste and the red wine, stirring

continuously for 2 minutes, or until the sauce has reduced. Add the beef, stir in the cream, then reduce the heat to medium–low and simmer gently for a further minute, or until the sauce has thickened. Serve with the fettuccine or tagliatelle.

NUTRITION PER SERVE
Fat 53.5 g; Protein 47 g; Carbohydrate 74 g; Dietary Fibre 5.5 g; Cholesterol 243 mg; 4085 kJ (975 Cal)

COOK'S FILE
Note: The sauce can be frozen. Thaw on a plate in the fridge for 4–5 hours.

1

3

TERIYAKI CHICKEN WITH GINGER CHIVE RICE

Preparation time: 10 minutes +
   1 hour marinating
Cooking time: 20 minutes
Serves 4

4 small chicken breast fillets, skin on
   (about 170 g each)
1/4 cup (60 ml) Japanese soy sauce
2 tablespoons sake
1 1/2 tablespoons mirin
1 1/2 tablespoons soft brown sugar
3 teaspoons finely grated fresh ginger
1 1/2 cups (300 g) long-grain rice
2 tablespoons finely chopped fresh
   chives
2 tablespoons oil

1 Pound each breast between two sheets of plastic wrap with a mallet or rolling pin until 1 cm thick.

2 Place the soy sauce, sake, mirin, sugar and 1 teaspoon of the ginger in a flat non-metallic dish big enough to fit all the chicken in a single layer and stir until the sugar has dissolved. Add the chicken and turn to coat. Cover and refrigerate for 1 hour, turning once halfway through.

3 Once the chicken has marinated, bring a large saucepan of water to the boil. Add the rice and cook for 12 minutes, stirring occasionally. Drain. Stir in the chives and the remaining ginger, then cover until ready to serve.

4 Meanwhile, drain the chicken, reserving the marinade. Heat the oil in a large deep frying pan and cook the chicken, skin-side-down over medium heat for 4–5 minutes, or until the skin is crisp. Turn and cook the other side for 4 minutes—remove from the pan (the chicken should not be quite cooked through).

5 Add the reserved marinade and 1/4 cup (60 ml) water to the pan and scrape any sediment stuck to the base. Bring to the boil over high heat, then return the chicken (skin-side-up) with any juices to the pan. Cook for 5–6 minutes, or until just cooked through, turning once to coat. (If the sauce is still a little runny, remove the chicken and boil the sauce over high heat until it is slightly syrupy.) Rest the chicken for a few minutes.

6 To serve, divide the rice among four serving plates and place the chicken (either whole or sliced on the diagonal) on top. Drizzle with a little sauce and serve with steamed Asian greens.

NUTRITION PER SERVE
Fat 27 g; Protein 39.5 g; Carbohydrate 66 g; Dietary Fibre 0.5 g; Cholesterol 124 mg; 2845 kJ (680 Cal)

CARAMEL PORK AND PUMPKIN STIR-FRY

Preparation time: 15 minutes
Cooking time: 20 minutes
Serves 4

1¼ cups (250 g) jasmine rice
300 g butternut pumpkin
500 g pork fillet
2 cloves garlic, crushed
2–3 tablespoons peanut oil
⅓ cup (60 g) soft brown sugar
¼ cup (60 ml) fish sauce
¼ cup (60 ml) rice vinegar
2 tablespoons chopped fresh
    coriander leaves
1.25 kg mixed Asian greens
    (bok choy, choy sum, gai larn)

1 Bring a large saucepan of water to the boil. Add the rice and cook for 12 minutes, stirring occasionally. Drain well.
2 Meanwhile, cut the pumpkin into pieces roughly 2 cm x 4 cm and 5 mm thick. Thinly slice the pork, then combine with the garlic and 2 teaspoons of the peanut oil. Season with salt and plenty of pepper.
3 Heat a wok until very hot, add 1 tablespoon oil and swirl to coat. When just starting to smoke, stir-fry the pork in two batches for about 1 minute per batch, or until the meat changes colour. Transfer to a plate. Add the remaining oil to the wok and stir-fry the pumpkin for 4 minutes, or until tender but not falling apart.

Remove and add to the pork.
4 Combine the sugar, fish sauce, rice vinegar and ½ cup (125 ml) water in the wok and boil for about 10 minutes, or until syrupy. Return the pork and pumpkin to the wok and stir for 1 minute, or until well coated and heated through. Stir in the coriander.
5 Place the mixed Asian greens in a paper-lined bamboo steamer over a wok of simmering water for 3 minutes, or until wilted. Serve immediately with the stir-fry and rice.

NUTRITION PER SERVE
Fat 15.5 g; Protein 38 g; Carbohydrate 73 g; Dietary Fibre 6 g; Cholesterol 118.5 mg; 2445 kJ (585 Cal)

3

4

SAUSAGES AND MASH WITH FRENCH SHALLOT GRAVY

Preparation time: 15 minutes
Cooking time: 25 minutes
Serves 4

1/3 cup (80 ml) olive oil
200 g French shallots, peeled and
    thinly sliced
1 tablespoon plain flour
1/2 cup (125 ml) red wine
1 1/2 cups (375 ml) good-quality
    beef stock
1 tablespoon Dijon mustard
1.5 kg potatoes, chopped
150 g butter
8 thick good-quality pork sausages
    (about 100 g each)
450 g green beans, top and tailed

1   Heat 2 tablespoons of the oil in a large frying pan over medium heat. Add the French shallots and cook for 5 minutes, stirring often until they soften and become transparent. Add the flour and cook for 30 seconds. Increase the heat to high, pour in the wine and stock and bring to the boil. Reduce the heat to medium and simmer for 10 minutes, or until the gravy thickens and reduces. Stir in the mustard, then reduce the heat to medium–low and simmer gently until the sausages and mash are ready.

2   Meanwhile, cook the potatoes in a large saucepan of boiling water for 12–15 minutes, or until tender. Drain and return to the pan with 1 tablespoon of olive oil and 120 g of the butter. Mash with a potato masher until smooth and creamy, then season to taste with salt and freshly ground black pepper.

3   While the potatoes are cooking, prick the sausages with a fork. Heat a large frying pan over medium–high heat, add a tablespoon of oil and add the sausages. Cook for 10 minutes, or until cooked through, turning often to brown evenly.

4   Bring a saucepan of lightly salted water to the boil, then add the beans and cook for 4 minutes, or until just tender. Whisk the remaining butter into the gravy and season. To serve, place a mound of mash on each plate, top with the sausages and gravy, and serve with the beans on the side.

NUTRITION PER SERVE
Fat 83 g; Protein 32.5 g; Carbohydrate 62 g; Dietary Fibre 11.5 g; Cholesterol 195 mg; 4780 kJ (1140 Cal)

COOK'S FILE
Note: To save time, slice 200 g red onions instead of the French shallots.

4

VEAL SCALOPPINE WITH SAGE

Preparation time: 15 minutes
Cooking time: 1 hour
Serves 4

600 g small new potatoes, halved
1/3 cup (80 ml) olive oil
8 small (600 g) veal scaloppine fillets or schnitzels
4 slices pancetta, cut in half lengthways
8 fresh sage leaves
1 cup (250 ml) Marsala
250 g asparagus spears

1 Preheat the oven to moderately hot 200°C (400°F/Gas 6). Cook the potatoes in a large saucepan of boiling water for 10 minutes. Drain and transfer to a baking tray with 2 tablespoons of the olive oil. Toss well and bake for 40–50 minutes, or until crisp.

2 Meanwhile, pound each veal fillet between two sheets of plastic wrap with a mallet or rolling pin until 5 mm thick. Press a piece of pancetta and a sage leaf onto each scaloppine fillet, then skewer with a toothpick. Season well with salt and freshly ground black pepper.

3 Heat the remaining oil in a large heavy-based frying pan. Place the scaloppine pancetta-side-down in the pan and cook for 1–2 minutes. Turn and cook for another minute. Remove from the pan and keep warm (you may have to do this in two batches). Add the Marsala and cook for 4–5 minutes, or until syrupy and reduced by half. Return the scaloppine to the pan and toss lightly in the sauce until warmed through.

4 When the potatoes are nearly ready, bring a large saucepan of lightly salted water to the boil. Add the asparagus and cook for 3 minutes. Drain.

5 To serve, remove the toothpicks from the scaloppine and divide among four serving plates. Drizzle any pan juices on top. Serve with the asparagus and roast potatoes on the side.

NUTRITION PER SERVE
Fat 24.5 g; Protein 39 g; Carbohydrate 29 g; Dietary Fibre 4 g; Cholesterol 134 mg; 2345 kJ (560 Cal)

2

PAN-FRIED LAMB FILLETS WITH RED WINE

Preparation time: 10 minutes
Cooking time: 20 minutes
Serves 4

600 g small new potatoes
160 g snow peas, trimmed
2 tablespoons olive oil
4 lamb backstraps or eye of loin fillets (about 200 g each), trimmed
2/3 cup (170 ml) red wine
1 tablespoon redcurrant jelly
2 teaspoons chopped fresh thyme
30 g butter, chilled and cut into cubes

1 Cook the potatoes in a large saucepan of lightly salted boiling water for 15–20 minutes, or until tender. Add the snow peas and cook for a further 1 minute. Drain the vegetables, return to the pan and toss gently with 1 tablespoon of the oil.

2 Meanwhile, heat the remaining oil in a large frying pan and cook the lamb fillets over medium–high heat for 4–5 minutes, or until cooked, but still pink inside. Remove from the pan, cover and keep warm.

3 Add the wine, redcurrant jelly and thyme to the pan and bring to the boil. Boil rapidly for 5 minutes, or until reduced and syrupy. Stir in the butter.

4 To serve, slice the lamb on the diagonal, divide among four plates and spoon some of the sauce on top. Serve with the vegetables.

NUTRITION PER SERVE
Fat 22 g; Protein 46 g; Carbohydrate 24 g; Dietary Fibre 4 g; Cholesterol 149 mg; 2130 kJ (510 Cal)

3

BEER-BATTERED FISH FILLETS WITH CHIPS

Preparation time: 15 minutes
Cooking time: 15 minutes
Serves 4

¹/4 cup (30 g) self-raising flour
¹/4 cup (30 g) cornflour
1 cup (125 g) plain flour
1 cup (250 ml) beer
oil, for deep-frying
4 large Pontiac potatoes, cut into
   finger-size chips
4 flathead fillets (about 200 g each),
   skinned and pin boned
2 lemons, cut into wedges

1 Preheat the oven to moderate 180°C (350°F/Gas 4). Sift the self-raising flour, cornflour and ¹/2 cup (60 g) of the plain flour into a large bowl and make a well in the centre. Gradually whisk in the beer to make a smooth batter. Cover.

2 Fill a large heavy-based saucepan one-third full of oil and heat to 180°C (350°F), or until a cube of bread dropped into the oil browns in 15 seconds. Deep-fry the potato chips in batches for 2–4 minutes, or until pale golden. Drain on paper towels. Deep-fry again for 3 minutes, or until golden and cooked through. Keep hot in the oven while you cook the fish.

3 Reheat the oil to 180°C (350°F). Stir the batter, then coat the fish fillets in the remaining plain flour, shaking off the excess. Dip the fillets into the batter, allowing the excess to drip off a little. Slowly ease the fillets into the hot oil, holding the tail out for a few seconds—turn with tongs if necessary. Cook for 4–5 minutes, or until golden brown and the fish is cooked through. Remove with a slotted spoon and drain on crumpled paper towels. Serve with the chips, lemon wedges and a green salad.

NUTRITION PER SERVE
Fat 30.5 g; Protein 51 g; Carbohydrate 61 g; Dietary Fibre 5.5 g; Cholesterol 114 mg; 3130 kJ (750 Cal)

COOK'S FILE
Hint: Use any type of white fish fillets (snapper, blue eye cod or John Dory) and any type of beer to vary the flavour.

1

3

LAMB, MINT AND CHILLI STIR-FRY

Preparation time: 10 minutes
Cooking time: 15 minutes
Serves 4

1¼ cups (250 g) jasmine rice
2 tablespoons oil
750 g lamb backstrap, sliced thinly
2 cloves garlic, finely chopped
1 small red onion, cut into wedges
1 fresh bird's eye chilli, finely chopped
¼ cup (60 ml) lime juice
2 tablespoons sweet chilli sauce
2 tablespoons fish sauce
½ cup (10 g) fresh mint leaves

1   Bring a large saucepan of water to the boil. Add the rice and cook for 12 minutes, stirring occasionally. Drain well.

2   Meanwhile, heat a wok until very hot, add 1 tablespoon oil and swirl to coat. Add the lamb in batches and cook for 2 minutes, or until browned. Remove from the wok.

3   Heat the remaining oil in the wok, add the garlic and onion and stir-fry for 1 minute, then add the chilli and cook for 30 seconds. Return the lamb to the wok, then add the lime juice, sweet chilli sauce and fish sauce and stir-fry for 2 minutes over high heat. Stir in the mint and serve with the rice.

NUTRITION PER SERVE
Fat 16.5 g; Protein 44 g; Carbohydrate 53 g; Dietary Fibre 2 g; Cholesterol 122 mg; 2270 kJ (540 Cal)

COOK'S FILE
Variation: Try chicken breasts or pork loin, adding ½ cup (80 g) cashews and basil instead of mint.

SALT AND PEPPER CHICKEN WITH ASIAN GREENS AND OYSTER SAUCE

Preparation time: 15 minutes
Cooking time: 20 minutes
Serves 4

1$^1/_4$ cups (250 g) jasmine rice
$^1/_3$ cup (40 g) plain flour
$^3/_4$ teaspoon five-spice powder
1$^1/_2$ teaspoons fine sea salt
1 teaspoon ground white pepper
750 g chicken breast fillets, cut into
    thin strips (1 cm x 5 cm)
145 ml peanut oil

1.25 kg mixed Asian greens
    (bok choy, choy sum or gai larn)
$^1/_2$ cup (125 ml) oyster sauce

1 Preheat the oven to moderately hot 200°C (400°F/Gas 6). Bring a large saucepan of water to the boil. Add the rice and cook for 12 minutes, stirring occasionally. Drain well.

2 Meanwhile, combine the flour, five-spice powder, salt and pepper in a large bowl. Toss the chicken strips in the flour until well coated. Heat $^1/_4$ cup (60 ml) of the oil in a large frying pan over medium–high heat. Add the chicken in three batches and cook, turning, for about 3 minutes, or until browned. Drain on crumpled paper towels and keep warm.

3 Heat the remaining oil and cook the mixed Asian greens over medium–high heat for 1–2 minutes. Add the oyster sauce and toss through. Serve on a bed of jasmine rice topped with the chicken strips.

NUTRITION PER SERVE
Fat 32.5 g; Protein 50 g; Carbohydrate 68 g; Dietary Fibre 5 g; Cholesterol 123.5 mg; 3195 kJ (765 Cal)

SALMON AND DILL POTATO PATTIES WITH LIME MAYONNAISE

Preparation time: 15 minutes
Cooking time: 25 minutes
Serves 4

400 g new potatoes (unpeeled optional), cut in half
2 teaspoons grated lime rind
1¼ cups (310 g) good-quality whole-egg mayonnaise
425 g can good-quality salmon, drained, bones removed
1 tablespoon chopped fresh dill
2 spring onions, thinly sliced
1 egg
1 cup (80 g) fresh breadcrumbs
¼ cup (60 ml) oil
200 g rocket leaves
lime wedges, to serve

1 Cook the potatoes in a large saucepan of boiling water for 12–15 minutes, or until tender. Drain well and cool.
2 Meanwhile, combine the lime rind and 1 cup (250 g) of the mayonnaise.
3 Transfer the potato to a large bowl, then mash roughly with the back of a spoon, leaving some large chunks. Stir in the salmon, dill and spring onion and season. Mix in the egg and the remaining mayonnaise. Divide into eight portions, forming palm-size patties. Press lightly into the breadcrumbs to coat.
4 Heat the oil in a non-stick frying pan and cook the patties, turning, for 3–4 minutes, or until golden brown. Drain on paper towels. Serve with a dollop of lime mayonnaise, rocket leaves and lime wedges.

NUTRITION PER SERVE
Fat 47.5 g; Protein 28 g; Carbohydrate 40 g; Dietary Fibre 4 g; Cholesterol 134 mg; 2900 kJ (690 Cal)

3

3

CHICKEN BREASTS WITH MUSTARD CREAM SAUCE

Preparation time: 10 minutes
Cooking time: 20 minutes
Serves 4

4 chicken breasts (about 200 g each)
2 tablespoons oil
1 clove garlic, crushed
1/4 cup (60 ml) white wine
2 tablespoons wholegrain mustard
2 teaspoons chopped fresh thyme
300 ml cream
240 g green beans, top and tailed
320 g baby yellow squash, halved

1 Pound each chicken breast between two sheets of plastic wrap with a mallet or rolling pin to about 1 cm thick.

2 Heat the oil in a frying pan over high heat. Add the chicken breasts and cook for 4–5 minutes on each side, or until brown. Remove and cover with foil.

3 Add the garlic to the frying pan and cook for 1 minute over medium heat, then stir in the wine, mustard and thyme. Increase the heat to medium–high and pour in the cream. Simmer for about 5 minutes, or until the sauce has reduced and thickened slightly, then season to taste.

4 Meanwhile, bring a saucepan of lightly salted water to the boil, add the beans and squash and cook for 2–4 minutes, or until just tender. Season to taste. To serve, pour a little of the sauce over the chicken and serve with the vegetables on the side.

NUTRITION PER SERVE
Fat 53.5 g; Protein 48 g; Carbohydrate 7 g; Dietary Fibre 4 g; Cholesterol 236 mg; 2950 kJ (705 Cal)

3

ORANGE SWEET POTATO, SPINACH AND WATER CHESTNUT STIR-FRY

Preparation time: 15 minutes
Cooking time: 20 minutes
Serves 4

1½ cups (300 g) long-grain rice
500 g orange sweet potato
1 tablespoon oil
2 cloves garlic, crushed
2 teaspoons sambal oelek
227 g can water chestnuts, sliced
2 teaspoons grated palm sugar
390 g English spinach, stems
    removed
2 tablespoons soy sauce
2 tablespoons vegetable stock

1 Bring a large saucepan of water to the boil. Add the rice and cook for 12 minutes, stirring occasionally. Drain well.

2 Meanwhile, cut the sweet potato into 1.5 cm x 1.5 cm cubes. Cook the sweet potato in a large saucepan of boiling water for 15 minutes, or until tender. Drain well.

3 Heat a wok until very hot, add the oil and swirl to coat. Stir-fry the garlic and sambal oelek for 1 minute, or until fragrant. Add the sweet potato and water chestnuts and stir-fry over medium–high heat for 2 minutes. Reduce the heat to medium, add the palm sugar and cook for a further 2 minutes, or until the sugar has melted. Add the spinach, soy sauce and stock and toss until the spinach has just wilted. Serve with the steamed rice.

NUTRITION PER SERVE
Fat 5.5 g; Protein 10.5 g; Carbohydrate 82 g; Dietary Fibre 6.5 g; Cholesterol 0 mg; 1785 kJ (425 Cal)

COOK'S FILE
Notes: Sambal oelek is made from mashed fresh red chillies mixed with salt and vinegar or tamarind.
Palm sugar is available from most large supermarkets in jars or wrapped in paper. Use demerara or soft brown sugar if not available.

3

LEMON GRASS BEEF

Preparation time: 15 minutes +
  10 minutes marinating
Cooking time: 25 minutes
Serves 4

1½ cups (300 g) long-grain rice
3 cloves garlic, finely chopped
1 tablespoon grated fresh ginger
4 stems lemon grass (white part only),
  finely chopped
2½ tablespoons oil
600 g lean rump steak, trimmed and
  sliced thinly across the grain
1 tablespoon lime juice
1–2 tablespoons fish sauce
2 tablespoons kecap manis
1 large red onion, cut into small
  wedges
200 g green beans, sliced on the
  diagonal into 5 cm lengths

1 Bring a large saucepan of water
to the boil. Add the rice and cook
for 12 minutes, stirring occasionally.
Drain well.
2 Meanwhile, combine the garlic,
ginger, lemon grass and 2 teaspoons
of the oil in a non-metallic bowl.
Add the beef, then marinate for
10 minutes. Combine the lime juice,
fish sauce and kecap manis.
3 Heat a wok until very hot, add
1 tablespoon oil and swirl to coat.
Stir-fry the beef in batches for
2–3 minutes, or until browned.
Remove from the wok.
4 Reheat the wok to very hot, heat
the remaining oil, then add the
onion and stir-fry for 2 minutes.
Add the beans and cook for another
2 minutes, then return the beef to the
wok. Pour in the fish sauce mixture
and cook until heated through. Serve
with the rice.

NUTRITION PER SERVE
Fat 19 g; Protein 40 g; Carbohydrate 63 g;
Dietary Fibre 3 g; Cholesterol 96 mg;
2460 kJ (590 Cal)

COOK'S FILE
Notes: Ensure your lemon grass is
fresh—the end of the stalk should not
be too dry and should still have a
strong lemon scent.
Kecap manis is a thick sweet soy sauce
available in the sauces or Asian food
section of your local supermarket. If not
available, use soy sauce sweetened
with a little soft brown sugar.

4

FISH FILLETS WITH FENNEL AND RED CAPSICUM SALSA

Preparation time: 10 minutes
Cooking time: 20 minutes
Serves 4

750 g small new potatoes
1 teaspoon fennel seeds
1/2 cup (125 ml) olive oil
2 tablespoons drained baby capers
1 small red capsicum, seeded and
    finely diced
250 g mixed salad leaves, washed
    and picked over
2 tablespoons balsamic vinegar
4 white fish fillets (blue eye cod or
    John Dory) (about 200 g each)

1 Cook the potatoes in a large saucepan of boiling water for 15–20 minutes, or until tender. Drain and keep warm.
2 Meanwhile, to make the salsa, place the fennel seeds in a dry frying pan and dry-fry over medium heat for 1 minute, or until fragrant. Remove the seeds from the pan. Heat 1 tablespoon of the oil in the same pan over medium heat. When the oil is hot but not smoking, add the capers and flash-fry for 1–2 minutes, or until crisp. Remove from the pan. Heat another tablespoon of oil, add the capsicum and cook, stirring, for 4–5 minutes, or until cooked through. Remove from the pan and combine with the fennel seeds and fried capers.
3 Place the salad leaves in a serving bowl. To make the dressing, combine the balsamic vinegar and 1/4 cup (60 ml) of the olive oil in a bowl. Add 1 tablespoon to the salsa, then toss the rest through the salad leaves.
4 Wipe the frying pan clean, then heat the remaining oil in the pan over medium–high heat. Season the fish fillets well with salt and freshly ground black pepper. When the oil is hot, but not smoking, cook the fish fillets for 2–3 minutes on each side (depending on thickness), or until cooked through. Serve the fillets immediately with the capsicum salsa, potatoes and salad.

NUTRITION PER SERVE
Fat 30 g; Protein 46.5 g; Carbohydrate 27 g; Dietary Fibre 5.5 g; Cholesterol 118 mg; 2365 kJ (565 Cal)

2

4

PORK WITH PAPRIKA, POTATOES AND SHALLOTS

Preparation time: 15 minutes
Cooking time: 45 minutes
Serves 4

1 tablespoon paprika
4 thick pork loin cutlets
2 tablespoons olive oil
1/4 cup (60 ml) sherry vinegar
1/4 teaspoon cayenne pepper
1/2 cup (125 ml) puréed tomato
400 g potatoes, cut into 2 cm cubes
8 French shallots, peeled
200 g rocket leaves

1 Combine the paprika with 1/4 teaspoon each of salt and freshly ground black pepper. Sprinkle over both sides of the pork. Heat the oil over medium heat in a deep frying pan large enough to fit the cutlets in a single layer and cook the cutlets until brown on both sides.

2 Pour the sherry vinegar into the pan and stir well to scrape up any sediment stuck to the base. Stir in the cayenne pepper, puréed tomato and 1 cup (250 ml) hot water. Bring to the boil, then add the potato and shallots. Reduce the heat and simmer, covered, for 30 minutes, or until the sauce has thickened and reduced by half—check the liquid level once or twice, and add a little more water if necessary. Season.

3 To serve, divide the rocket leaves among four serving plates and place a cutlet on top. Spoon the sauce and potatoes over the top.

NUTRITION PER SERVE
Fat 17 g; Protein 40.5 g; Carbohydrate 17 g; Dietary Fibre 3.5 g; Cholesterol 102.5 mg; 1615 kJ (385 Cal)

SEARED SALMON WITH SESAME AND CUCUMBER NOODLES

Preparation time: 15 minutes +
  2 hours refrigeration
Cooking time: 10 minutes
Serves 4

250 g buckwheat soba noodles
1½ tablespoons sesame oil
2 tablespoons kecap manis
1 tablespoon Chinese black vinegar
2 Lebanese cucumbers, julienned
6 spring onions, trimmed and sliced
  on the diagonal into 4 cm lengths

2 tablespoons black sesame seeds
600 g salmon fillet pieces, skinned
  and boned

1 Cook the noodles in a large saucepan of boiling water according to the packet instructions until tender—this should take about 5 minutes. Drain well. Place in a large bowl and mix in 2 teaspoons of the sesame oil, then set aside to cool. Combine the kecap manis, vinegar and the remaining sesame oil, then toss 1 tablespoon of the mixture through the noodles. Cover the noodles and refrigerate for about 2 hours.

2 About 20 minutes before serving, remove the noodles from the refrigerator and gently mix in the cucumber, spring onion and black sesame seeds.

3 Heat a large frying pan over medium–high heat. Brush the salmon pieces lightly with oil and season with salt and freshly ground black pepper. Cook for 1–2 minutes on each side, or until cooked to your liking. Remove from the heat and allow to cool until cool enough to handle. Flake the fish into large pieces and gently incorporate it into the noodles, along with the rest of the dressing—be careful not to over-handle or the salmon will flake into small pieces. Serve immediately.

NUTRITION PER SERVE
Fat 21 g; Protein 40.5 g; Carbohydrate 49 g;
Dietary Fibre 3 g; Cholesterol 78 mg;
2230 kJ (535 Cal)

2

3

PRAWNS WITH SPICY TAMARIND SAUCE

Preparation time: 15 minutes
Cooking time: 25 minutes
Serves 4

½ cup (80 g) raw cashew nuts
1¼ cups (250 g) jasmine rice
2 garlic cloves, finely chopped
1½ tablespoons fish sauce
1 tablespoon sambal oelek
1 tablespoon peanut oil
1 kg raw medium prawns, peeled
   and deveined with tails intact
2 teaspoons tamarind concentrate
1½ tablespoons grated palm sugar
350 g choy sum, cut into 10 cm
   lengths

1 Preheat the oven to moderate 180°C (350°F/Gas 4). Spread the cashews on a baking tray and bake for 5–8 minutes, or until lightly golden—watch carefully, as they will burn easily.

2 Meanwhile, bring a large saucepan of water to the boil. Add the rice and cook for 12 minutes, stirring occasionally. Drain well.

3 Place the garlic, fish sauce, sambal oelek and toasted cashews in a blender or food processor, adding 2–3 tablespoons of water, if needed, and blend to a rough paste.

4 Heat a wok until very hot, add the oil and swirl to coat. Add the prawns, toss for 1–2 minutes, or until starting to turn pink. Remove from the wok. Add the cashew paste and stir-fry for 1 minute, or until it starts to brown slightly. Add the tamarind, sugar and about ⅓ cup (80 ml) water, then bring to the boil, stirring well. Return the prawns to the wok and stir to coat. Cook for 2–3 minutes, or until the prawns are cooked through.

5 Place the choy sum in a paper-lined bamboo steamer and steam over a wok or saucepan of simmering water for 3 minutes, or until tender. Serve with the prawns and rice.

NUTRITION PER SERVE
Fat 14.5 g; Protein 35 g; Carbohydrate 60 g; Dietary Fibre 3.5 g; Cholesterol 186.5 mg; 2135 kJ (510 Cal)

COOK'S FILE
Note: To save time, you can purchase pre-peeled raw prawns with the tails intact. You will only need 500 g as the shells make up roughly half the weight of the prawns.

4

PORK CHOPS WITH APPLE AND RED ONION CHUTNEY

Preparation time: 15 minutes
Cooking time: 30 minutes
Serves 4

125 g butter
2 small red onions, sliced
2 Granny Smith apples, peeled, cored, then cut into quarters and sliced
1/4 teaspoon ground cloves
1/3 cup (115 g) honey
4 pork loin chops (about 250 g each)
2 teaspoons oil
1/2 teaspoon caraway seeds
725 g green cabbage, thinly shredded

1 To make the chutney, melt 50 g of the butter in a saucepan, then add the onion, apple, cloves and honey. Simmer, covered, for 10 minutes over low heat. Increase the heat to medium and cook, uncovered, for a further 20 minutes, or until the liquid is reduced to a thick chutney. Allow to cool.

2 Meanwhile, season the chops well on both sides with salt and freshly ground black pepper. Heat the oil and 50 g of the butter in a large frying pan and sauté the chops over medium–high heat for 6–8 minutes on each side, or until browned and cooked through. Remove the pan from the heat, leaving the chops to rest for 2 minutes.

3 Melt the remaining butter in a large saucepan, add the caraway seeds and green cabbage and cook, covered, over medium–low heat, tossing a few times with tongs, for 12 minutes, or until tender.

4 To serve, place a pork chop on each serving plate and serve the cabbage on the side. Dollop with a spoonful of chutney.

NUTRITION PER SERVE
Fat 35.5 g; Protein 55 g; Carbohydrate 41 g; Dietary Fibre 8.5 g; Cholesterol 222 mg; 2885 kJ (690 Cal)

COOK'S FILE
Note: Resting the chops for a couple of minutes before serving allows the juices to settle evenly throughout the chop, resulting in lovely moist meat.

VEAL SCHNITZEL WITH DILL POTATO SALAD

Preparation time: 15 minutes
Cooking time: 25 minutes
Serves 4

750 g desiree potatoes, unpeeled
500 g veal leg steaks
1/2 cup (60 g) seasoned plain flour
2 eggs, lightly beaten
1 cup (100 g) dry breadcrumbs
1/2 cup (125 ml) virgin olive oil
2 tablespoons lemon juice
1 1/2 tablespoons finely chopped
    fresh dill
200 g mixed salad leaves

1 Cook the potatoes in a large saucepan of boiling water for 15–20 minutes, or until tender. Drain. Cut into quarters lengthways and cover to keep warm.

2 Meanwhile, beat the veal between two sheets of plastic wrap to 5 mm thickness. Coat the veal in the flour and shake off the excess. Dip the veal in the egg, then coat in breadcrumbs. Place the schnitzel on a flat tray, cover and freeze for 5 minutes.

3 Heat 1/4 cup (60 ml) of the oil in a large frying pan and cook the veal in two batches, over medium–high heat for 2–3 minutes on each side, or until golden and cooked through. Drain on crumpled paper towels and keep warm.

4 Whisk the lemon juice, dill and remaining oil together in a small bowl and pour over the potatoes. Season with salt and freshly ground black pepper and toss gently. Serve the schnitzel with the potatoes and a mixed salad.

NUTRITION PER SERVE
Fat 34.5 g; Protein 41 g; Carbohydrate 53 g; Dietary Fibre 6.5 g; Cholesterol 203.5 mg; 2875 kJ (685 Cal)

COOK'S FILE
Hint: Snip the edges of the veal with scissors to prevent the sides curling during cooking.

SPRING ONION LAMB

Preparation time: 10 minutes +
　10 minutes marinating
Cooking time: 30 minutes
Serves 4

600 g lean lamb backstraps
1 tablespoon Chinese rice wine
　or dry sherry
1/4 cup (60 ml) soy sauce
1/2 teaspoon white pepper
6 spring onions
11/2 cups (300 g) long-grain rice
2 tablespoons oil
750 g choy sum, cut into 10 cm
　lengths
3 cloves garlic, crushed
1 tablespoon Chinese black vinegar
1 teaspoon sesame oil

3

1 Slice the lamb backstrap across the grain into very thin slices. Place in a non-metallic bowl with the rice wine, 1 tablespoon of the soy sauce, 1/2 teaspoon salt and the white pepper and mix well. Cover and refrigerate for 10 minutes. Slice the spring onions diagonally into 4 cm lengths.
2 Meanwhile, bring a large saucepan of water to the boil. Add the rice and cook for 12 minutes, stirring occasionally. Drain.
3 Heat a wok over high heat, add 1/2 tablespoon oil and swirl to coat. Add the choy sum, stir-fry quickly, then add 1 clove of the crushed garlic and 1 tablespoon soy sauce. Cook for 3 minutes, or until cooked, but crisp. Immediately take the wok off the heat, remove the greens and keep warm.
4 Wipe the wok clean and heat over high heat, then add 1 tablespoon oil and swirl to coat. Add the lamb in

two batches and stir-fry quickly over high heat for 1–2 minutes, or until brown. Remove from the wok.
5 Add a little more oil to the wok, if necessary. Add the spring onion and remaining garlic and stir-fry for 1–2 minutes. Combine the vinegar, sesame oil and the remaining soy sauce. Pour into the wok, stirring for 1 minute, or until combined. Return the lamb to the wok and continue to stir-fry for another minute, or until combined and heated through. Serve immediately with the stir-fried greens and rice.

NUTRITION PER SERVE
Fat 19 g; Protein 38.5 g; Carbohydrate 63 g; Dietary Fibre 4 g; Cholesterol 100.5 mg; 2450 kJ (585 Cal)

COOK'S FILE
Note: Chinese rice wine and Chinese black vinegar are available in Asian grocery stores.

2

3

GINGER CHICKEN STIR-FRY WITH HOKKIEN NOODLES

Preparation time: 15 minutes +
    5 minutes soaking
Cooking time: 10 minutes
Serves 4

2¹/₂ tablespoons finely shredded
    fresh ginger
¹/₄ cup (60 ml) mirin
2 tablespoons soy sauce
600 g chicken tenderloins or chicken
    breast fillets, cut diagonally into
    thin strips
180 g fresh baby corn
350 g choy sum
150 g fresh oyster mushrooms
500 g Hokkien noodles, gently
    separated
2 tablespoons oil
2 tablespoons oyster sauce

1   Combine the ginger, mirin and soy sauce in a non-metallic bowl. Add the chicken, coat well, then marinate while preparing the vegetables.

2   Cut the corn in half lengthways; trim the ends off the choy sum and cut into 6 cm lengths. If the mushrooms are very large, cut them in half. Soak the noodles in a large heatproof bowl in boiling water for 5 minutes. Drain and refresh under cold running water.

3   Heat a wok until very hot, add 1 tablespoon of the oil and swirl to coat. Remove the chicken from the marinade with a slotted spoon and cook in two batches over very high heat for 2 minutes, or until brown and just cooked. Remove from the wok.

4   Add the remaining oil to the wok and stir-fry the mushrooms and corn for 1–2 minutes, or until just softened. Add the remaining marinade, bring to the boil, then add the chicken, choy sum and noodles. Stir in the oyster sauce and cook, tossing well, for 1–2 minutes, or until the choy sum has wilted slightly and the noodles are warmed through.

NUTRITION PER SERVE
Fat 19.5 g; Protein 49 g; Carbohydrate 77 g;
Dietary Fibre 7 g; Cholesterol 115 mg;
2925 kJ (700 Cal)

TUNA STEAKS WITH OLIVE MAYONNAISE AND POTATO WEDGES

Preparation time: 15 minutes
Cooking time: 50 minutes
Serves 4

3 large Pontiac potatoes, unpeeled and cut lengthways into 8 wedges
345 ml olive oil
2 egg yolks, at room temperature
25 ml lemon juice
1/3 cup (40 g) pitted black olives, finely chopped
200 g baby rocket leaves
1 tablespoon finely chopped fresh rosemary
4 tuna steaks (about 200 g each)

1 Preheat the oven to moderately hot 200°C (400°F/Gas 6). Place the potatoes in a roasting tin and toss in 2 tablespoons of the oil. Bake for 45–50 minutes, or until crisp and golden.
2 Meanwhile, process the egg yolks in a food processor, adding 1/4 cup (60 ml) of the oil drop by drop. With the motor running, pour in 3/4 cup (185 ml) of the oil in a thin stream until the mixture thickens and becomes creamy. With the motor still running, add 1 teaspoon of the lemon juice, season with salt and blend for 30 seconds. Stir in the olives, cover and refrigerate.
3 To make the salad, toss the rocket leaves, 2 tablespoons of the oil and 1 tablespoon of the lemon juice together in a serving bowl.
4 Press the chopped rosemary into the tuna steaks. Heat the remaining tablespoon of oil in a large frying pan and sear the tuna steaks over medium–high heat for 2–3 minutes on each side, or until cooked to your liking. Serve with a dollop of olive mayonnaise, potato wedges and rocket salad.

NUTRITION PER SERVE
Fat 39.5 g; Protein 56 g; Carbohydrate 23 g; Dietary Fibre 4 g; Cholesterol 95.5 mg; 2815 kJ (675 Cal)

COOK'S FILE
Note: To save time, use 1 cup (250 g) of good-quality whole-egg mayonnaise instead of making your own.
Storage: Any remaining mayonnaise can be refrigerated for up to 2 days.

1

4

PARMESAN CHICKEN WITH QUICK SALSA VERDE

Preparation time: 15 minutes +
10 minutes refrigeration
Cooking time: 15 minutes
Serves 4

3 eggs
1 cup (30 g) loosely packed
fresh basil
2 tablespoons capers, rinsed
1 tablespoon Dijon mustard
2 tablespoons freshly grated
Parmesan
3/4 cup (185 ml) olive oil
1 cup (100 g) dry breadcrumbs
4 chicken breast fillets
(about 120 g each)
150 g rocket leaves
lemon wedges, to serve

1 Place 1 egg in a saucepan of cold water, bring to the boil and cook for 1 minute. Remove from the heat and refresh under cold water. Peel, then place in a food processor with the basil, capers, mustard and 1 tablespoon of the Parmesan, until combined. Gradually add 1/4 cup (60 ml) of the olive oil and process until you have a coarse sauce, taking care not to overprocess.

2 Beat the remaining eggs together with 1 tablespoon water. Combine the breadcrumbs with the remaining Parmesan on a plate. Pound each chicken breast between two sheets of plastic wrap with a mallet or rolling pin until 5 mm thick. Dip the chicken in the egg mixture, then coat in the breadcrumb mixture. Place on a paper-lined baking tray and refrigerate for 10 minutes, or until needed.

3 Heat the remaining oil in a large frying pan over high heat. Cook the chicken breasts in batches for 2–3 minutes each batch, or until golden on both sides and cooked through—keep warm between batches. Serve with the salsa verde, rocket leaves and lemon wedges.

NUTRITION PER SERVE
Fat 47 g; Protein 37 g; Carbohydrate 18.5 g; Dietary Fibre 2 g; Cholesterol 234.5 mg; 2685 kJ (640 Cal)

EASY STEWS AND CASSEROLES

BRAISED LAMB SHANKS IN RICH TOMATO SAUCE ON POLENTA

Preparation time: 10 minutes
Cooking time: 2 hours 30 minutes
Serves 4

2 tablespoons olive oil
1 large red onion, sliced
4 French-trimmed lamb shanks
    (about 250 g each)
2 cloves garlic, crushed
400 g can peeled chopped tomatoes
1/2 cup (125 ml) red wine
2 teaspoons chopped fresh rosemary
1 cup (150 g) instant polenta
50 g butter
1/2 cup (50 g) grated Parmesan

1 Preheat the oven to warm 160°C (315°F/Gas 2–3). Heat the oil in a 4 litre flameproof casserole dish over medium heat and sauté the onion for 3–4 minutes, or until softening and becoming transparent. Add the lamb shanks and cook for 2–3 minutes, or until lightly browned. Add the garlic, tomato and wine, then bring to the boil and cook for 3–4 minutes. Stir in the rosemary. Season with 1/4 teaspoon each of salt and pepper.
2 Cover, transfer to the oven and cook for 2 hours. Remove the lid, return to the oven and simmer for a further 15 minutes, or until the lamb just starts to fall off the bone. Check periodically that the sauce is not too dry, adding water if needed.
3 About 20 minutes before serving, bring 1 litre water to the boil in a saucepan. Add the polenta in a thin stream, whisking continuously, then reduce the heat to very low. Simmer for 8–10 minutes, or until thick and coming away from the side of the saucepan. Stir in the butter and Parmesan. To serve, spoon the polenta onto serving plates, top with the shanks and a little sauce from the casserole over the shanks.

NUTRITION PER SERVE
Fat 36.5 g; Protein 39 g; Carbohydrate 31 g; Dietary Fibre 3 g; Cholesterol 137 mg; 2615 kJ (625 Cal)

3

BEEF AND RED WINE STEW

Preparation time: 10 minutes
Cooking time: 2 hours
Serves 4

1 kg diced beef
¼ cup (30 g) seasoned plain flour
1 tablespoon oil
150 g bacon, diced
8 bulb spring onions, greens
    trimmed to 2 cm
200 g button mushrooms
2 cups (500 ml) red wine
2 tablespoons tomato paste
2 cups (500 ml) beef stock
1 bouquet garni (see Note)

1 Toss the beef in the seasoned flour until evenly coated, shaking off any excess. Heat the oil in a large saucepan over high heat. Cook the beef in three batches for about 3 minutes, or until well browned all over, adding a little extra oil as needed. Remove from the pan.

2 Add the bacon to the pan and cook for 2 minutes, or until browned. Remove with a slotted spoon and add to the beef. Add the spring onions and mushrooms and cook for 5 minutes, or until the onions are browned. Remove.

3 Slowly pour the red wine into the pan, scraping up any sediment from the bottom with a wooden spoon. Stir in the tomato paste and stock. Add the bouquet garni and return the beef, bacon and any juices. Bring to the boil, then reduce the heat and simmer for 45 minutes, then return the spring onions and mushrooms to the pan. Cook for 1 hour, or until the meat is very tender and the sauce is glossy. Serve with steamed new potatoes or mash.

NUTRITION PER SERVE
Fat 20 g; Protein 65 g; Carbohydrate 9.5 g; Dietary Fibre 3 g; Cholesterol 168.5 mg; 2363 kJ (563 Cal)

COOK'S FILE
Note: To make a bouquet garni, wrap the green part of a leek around a bay leaf, a sprig of thyme, a sprig of parsley and celery leaves, and tie with string. The combination of herbs can be varied according to taste.

1

3

THAI GREEN CHICKEN CURRY WITH CORIANDER RICE

Preparation time: 10 minutes
Cooking time: 20 minutes
Serves 4

1¼ cups (250 g) jasmine rice
1 tablespoon vegetable oil
1–2 tablespoons good-quality
  Thai green curry paste
4 fresh kaffir lime leaves
1 tablespoon fish sauce
2 teaspoons palm sugar
400 ml can coconut cream
750 g skinless chicken breast fillets,
  cut into strips (2 cm x 6 cm)
4 tablespoons roughly chopped fresh
  coriander leaves
2 tablespoons whole coriander leaves

1 Bring a large saucepan of water to the boil. Add the rice and cook for 12 minutes, stirring occasionally. Drain well.

2 Meanwhile, heat the oil over high heat in a wok, then add the curry paste and lime leaves and fry over medium–high heat for 1–2 minutes, or until fragrant. Add the fish sauce and palm sugar and mix well. Pour in the coconut cream, bring to the boil, then add the chicken strips.

Reduce the heat to medium and simmer for 12–15 minutes, or until the sauce is reduced and the chicken is tender and cooked through.

3 Just before serving, stir the chopped coriander through the rice. Serve the curry over the coriander rice, garnished with a few whole coriander leaves.

NUTRITION PER SERVE
Fat 38.5 g; Protein 47 g; Carbohydrate 56 g; Dietary Fibre 3.5 g; Cholesterol 124 mg; 3170 kJ (760 Cal)

2

2

BEEF MASALA WITH COCONUT RICE

Preparation time: 15 minutes +
  10 minutes standing
Cooking time: 1 hour 50 minutes
Serves 4

1 tablespoon oil
1 kg chuck beef, trimmed and
  cut into 2 cm cubes
1 large onion, thinly sliced
3 cloves garlic, chopped
1/3 cup (80 g) tikka masala
  curry paste
2 teaspoons tamarind concentrate
2 x 400 ml cans coconut milk
4 fresh curry leaves
1 1/2 cups (300 g) jasmine rice

1 To make the beef masala, heat the oil in a large saucepan over high heat. Add the meat and cook in three batches, for 4 minutes per batch, or until evenly browned. Remove from the pan.

2 Reduce the heat to medium, add the onion and cook for 5 minutes. Add the garlic and cook for 1 minute. Stir in the curry paste and tamarind and cook for 30–60 seconds, or until fragrant. Return the beef to the pan, add 550 ml coconut milk and the curry leaves and bring to the boil. Reduce the heat and simmer gently for 1 hour 30 minutes, or until the meat is tender and the sauce has reduced. Check occasionally to ensure that the sauce doesn't stick to the bottom of the pan—add some water if necessary.

3 Meanwhile, to make the coconut rice, wash and thoroughly drain the rice. Place the rice, the remaining coconut milk and 1 cup (250 ml) water in a saucepan. Bring slowly to the boil, stirring constantly, and boil for 1 minute. Reduce the heat to low and cook, covered tightly, for 20 minutes. Remove from the heat and leave, covered, for 10 minutes. Fluff the rice with a fork before serving. To serve, season the curry to taste, remove the curry leaves, if desired, and serve with the rice.

NUTRITION PER SERVE
Fat 59 g; Protein 63 g; Carbohydrate 72.5 g; Dietary Fibre 6 g; Cholesterol 148 mg; 4470 kJ (1070 Cal)

CHICKEN AND CIDER STEW WITH APPLE AND POTATO MASH

Preparation time: 15 minutes
Cooking time: 55 minutes
Serves 4

1 kg chicken thigh fillets, trimmed and cut into 2 cm cubes
1¹/₂ tablespoons finely chopped fresh thyme
1 tablespoon oil
90 g butter
3 French shallots, thinly sliced
1¹/₂ cups (375 ml) apple cider
1 kg potatoes, cubed
2 large green apples, peeled, cored and sliced into eighths
²/₃ cup (170 ml) cream

1 Season the chicken thighs with 2 teaspoons of the thyme and salt and black pepper. Heat the oil and 20 g of the butter in a large saucepan over medium–high heat. Cook the chicken in two batches for 2–3 minutes, or until evenly browned. Remove from the pan.

2 Add the French shallots and the remaining thyme to the pan and sauté for 2 minutes. Pour in the cider, then bring to the boil, scraping off any sediment that has stuck to the bottom of the pan. Return the chicken to the pan and cover. Reduce the heat to medium–low and cook for 35–40 minutes, or until the chicken is tender and the sauce has reduced (check occasionally to see if any water needs to be added).

3 Meanwhile, cook the potato and apple in a saucepan of boiling water for 15–20 minutes, or until tender. Drain and return to the pan over low heat for a minute to allow any water to evaporate. Remove from the heat, and mash with a potato masher. Stir in 2 tablespoons of the cream and the remaining butter with a wooden spoon, then season well with salt and pepper.

4 Gently stir the remaining cream into the chicken stew and cook for a further 2–4 minutes, or until the sauce has thickened. Serve at once with the potato and apple mash and a crisp green salad.

NUTRITION PER SERVE
Fat 59.5 g; Protein 54 g; Carbohydrate 56 g; Dietary Fibre 6 g; Cholesterol 333 mg; 4055 kJ (970 Cal)

2

2

3

MOROCCAN CHICKEN

Preparation time: 10 minutes +
    5 minutes standing
Cooking time: 35 minutes
Serves 4

1 tablespoon Moroccan spice blend
800 g chicken thigh fillets, trimmed
    and halved
1 tablespoon oil
60 g butter
1 large onion, cut into wedges
1 cinnamon stick
2 cloves garlic, crushed
2 tablespoons lemon juice plus
    wedges, to serve
1 cup (250 ml) chicken stock
1/3 cup (75 g) pitted prunes, halved
1 1/2 cups (225 g) couscous

1 Sprinkle half the spice blend over the chicken. Heat the oil and 20 g of the butter in a large saucepan or deep-sided frying pan over medium heat. Cook the chicken in batches for 5 minutes, or until evenly browned. Remove from the pan, then add the onion and cinnamon stick and cook for 2–3 minutes before adding the garlic. Return the chicken to the pan and add the lemon juice and the remaining spice mix. Season to taste, then cook, covered, for 5 minutes.

2 Add the stock and prunes to the pan and bring to the boil. Reduce the heat to medium–low and cook, uncovered, for 15 minutes, or until the chicken is cooked and the liquid has reduced to a sauce. Before serving, stir 20 g of the butter into the sauce.

3 About 10 minutes before the chicken is ready, place the couscous in a heatproof bowl, add 1 1/2 cups (375 ml) boiling water, and stand for 3–5 minutes. Stir in the remaining butter and fluff with a fork until the butter has melted and the grains separate. Serve with the chicken.

NUTRITION PER SERVE
Fat 32 g; Protein 46.5 g; Carbohydrate 56 g; Dietary Fibre 3 g; Cholesterol 212.5 mg; 2905 kJ (695 Cal)

COOK'S FILE
Note: Depending on the quality and freshness of the Moroccan spice blend you buy, you may need to use a little more then specified in the recipe.

1

VEGETABLE TAGINE WITH COUSCOUS

Preparation time: 15 minutes +
5 minutes standing
Cooking time: 40 minutes
Serves 4

¼ cup (60 ml) olive oil
1 large red capsicum, seeded and
cut into quarters
1 large eggplant, sliced into 1 cm
rounds, then in half again
400 g can chopped tomatoes
1 tablespoon harissa paste (see Note)
1 tablespoon Moroccan spice blend
1 cup (250 ml) vegetable stock
2 large zucchini, cut into 2 cm
chunks
1½ cups (225 g) couscous
20 g butter

1 Heat 1 tablespoon of the oil in a saucepan over medium–high heat. Sauté the capsicum, skin-side-down, covered, for 3–4 minutes, or until the skin is well browned. Remove from the pan. Peel off the skin and cut the flesh into 1 cm slices. Heat the remaining oil in the pan and cook the eggplant in batches over medium–high heat for 4–5 minutes, or until well browned. Remove.
2 Return the capsicum to the pan, then stir in the tomato, harissa paste and Moroccan spice blend. Pour in the stock and bring to the boil. Reduce the heat to medium–low and simmer, uncovered, for 15 minutes. Add the zucchini and eggplant and cook for a further 8 minutes, or until the vegetables are tender.
3 About 10 minutes before the vegetables are ready, place the couscous in a heatproof bowl, add 1½ cups (375 ml) boiling water,

and leave for 3–5 minutes. Stir in the butter and fluff with a fork until the butter has melted and the grains separate. Serve the vegetable tagine with the couscous.

NUTRITION PER SERVE
Fat 19 g; Protein 11 g; Carbohydrate 51.5 g; Dietary Fibre 5.5 g; Cholesterol 13 mg; 1765 kJ (420 Cal)

COOK'S FILE
Note: Harissa is a blend of chillies, garlic, spices and oil available at delicatessens or specialist food stores.

3

SICHUAN CHICKEN

Preparation time: 10 minutes
Cooking time: 25 minutes
Serves 4

1/4 teaspoon five-spice powder
750 g chicken thigh fillets, halved
2 tablespoons peanut oil
1 tablespoon julienned fresh ginger
1 teaspoon Sichuan peppercorns, crushed
1 teaspoon chilli bean paste (toban djan)
2 tablespoons light soy sauce
1 tablespoon Chinese rice wine
1 1/4 cups (250 g) jasmine rice
600 g baby bok choy, leaves separated

1 Sprinkle the five-spice powder over the chicken. Heat a wok until very hot, add half the oil and swirl to coat. Add the chicken and cook for 2 minutes each side, or until browned. Remove from the wok.

2 Reduce the heat to medium and cook the ginger for 30 seconds. Add the peppercorns and chilli bean paste. Return the chicken to the wok, add the soy sauce, wine and 1/2 cup (125 ml) water, then simmer for 15–20 minutes, or until cooked.

3 Meanwhile, bring a large saucepan of water to the boil. Add the rice and cook for 12 minutes, stirring occasionally. Drain well.

4 Heat the remaining oil in a saucepan. Add the bok choy and toss gently for 1 minute, or until the leaves wilt and the stems are tender. Serve with the chicken and rice.

NUTRITION PER SERVE
Fat 23.5 g; Protein 42 g; Carbohydrate 52 g; Dietary Fibre 2.5 g; Cholesterol 163 mg; 2465 kJ (590 Cal)

CHILLI CON CARNE

Preparation time: 15 minutes
Cooking time: 45 minutes
Serves 4

1 tablespoon oil
1 large red onion, finely chopped
2 cloves garlic, crushed
1½ teaspoons chilli powder
1 teaspoon ground oregano
2 teaspoons ground cumin
500 g lean beef mince
2 x 400 g cans chopped tomatoes
420 g can red kidney beans, drained and rinsed
8 flour tortillas
sour cream, to serve, optional

1 Preheat the oven to moderate 180°C (350°F/Gas 4). Heat the oil in a large saucepan, add the onion and garlic and cook, stirring, over medium heat for about 5 minutes, or until softened. Add the chilli powder, oregano and cumin and stir until fragrant. Add the mince and cook, stirring, for about 5 minutes, or until browned all over, breaking up any lumps with the back of a wooden spoon.

2 Add the tomato, beans and ½ cup (125 ml) water and simmer, stirring occasionally, for about 30 minutes, or until thick. Season to taste with salt and pepper. About 10 minutes before serving, wrap the tortillas in foil and heat them in the oven according to packet instructions to soften. Fill the tortillas with the chilli and wrap. Serve with sour cream and, if desired, a green salad.

NUTRITION PER SERVE
Fat 17 g; Protein 36 g; Carbohydrate 39.5 g; Dietary Fibre 9.5 g; Cholesterol 63.5 mg; 1915 kJ (460 Cal)

COOK'S FILE
Variations: Top jacket potatoes with chilli con carne and a dollop of sour cream, or serve with rice.

COCONUT BEEF CURRY ON TURMERIC RICE

Preparation time: 10 minutes +
    10 minutes standing
Cooking time: 1 hour 50 minutes
Serves 4

2 tablespoons oil
1 large onion, sliced
2 tablespoons good-quality vindaloo
    curry paste
1 kg chuck steak, trimmed and
    cubed
1 cup (250 ml) beef stock
200 ml coconut cream
1¼ cups (250 g) basmati rice
¾ teaspoon ground turmeric

1 Heat the oil in a large saucepan over medium–high heat. Add the onion and cook for 4–5 minutes, or until starting to soften. Add the curry paste and stir for 1 minute, or until fragrant. Add the steak and brown evenly for about 5 minutes.
2 Pour in the stock and bring to the boil. Reduce the heat to very low and simmer, covered, for 1 hour, or until the meat is tender. Remove the lid and cook for an extra 15 minutes to reduce the sauce.
3 Add the coconut cream, return to the boil, then simmer over low heat for a further 15–20 minutes, or until the beef is tender and the sauce has reduced.
4 About 25 minutes before the beef is ready, rinse the rice and place it in a large saucepan. Add the turmeric and 1¾ cups (440 ml) water and bring to the boil. Reduce the heat to very low, then cook, covered, for 10 minutes. Remove from the heat and leave to stand, covered, for 10 minutes. Divide the rice among four wide serving bowls and top with the beef curry.

NUTRITION PER SERVE
Fat 35.5 g; Protein 60 g; Carbohydrate 56 g;
Dietary Fibre 3 g; Cholesterol 147.5 mg;
3255 kJ (775 Cal)

COOK'S FILE
Variation: Use chicken thighs on the bone instead of beef, if desired. Reduce the cooking time by 30 minutes and serve when the chicken is starting to fall off the bone.

LAMB KOFTA CURRY

Preparation time: 15 minutes
Cooking time: 30 minutes
Serves 4

1¼ cups (250 g) jasmine rice
1 kg lean lamb mince
1 egg, lightly beaten
2 onions, finely chopped
120 g good-quality mild Korma
    curry paste
4 tablespoons chopped fresh
    coriander leaves
2 cloves garlic, crushed
2 tablespoons oil
400 g can diced tomatoes

1 Preheat the oven to hot 220°C (425°F/Gas 7) and lightly grease two baking trays. Bring a large saucepan of water to the boil. Add the rice and cook for 12 minutes, stirring occasionally. Drain well.

2 Meanwhile, combine the mince, egg, 1 of the onions, 2 tablespoons of the curry paste, 3 tablespoons of the coriander, 1 clove of garlic and salt. Form tablespoons of the mixture into balls and place on one of the prepared baking trays.

3 Heat 1 tablespoon of the oil in a large non-stick frying pan over medium heat. When hot, cook the balls in batches for 1 minute on each side, or until evenly golden, but not cooked through. Place on the second tray and bake for 5–7 minutes, or until cooked through.

4 Meanwhile, wipe the pan clean with paper towels. Heat the remaining oil over medium heat. Add the remaining onion and garlic and cook for 3 minutes, or until the onion is soft. Add the remaining curry paste and cook for 1 minute before adding the tomatoes and 1 cup (250 ml) water. Bring to the boil, then reduce the heat to low and gently simmer for 10 minutes, or until the sauce thickens slightly. Season with salt.

5 Add the baked meatballs and their juices to the sauce, and gently stir, coating in the sauce. Simmer for 5 minutes, or until the meatballs are warmed through. Serve with rice and sprinkle with the remaining coriander.

NUTRITION PER SERVE
Fat 37.5 g; Protein 60 g; Carbohydrate 58 g; Dietary Fibre 6 g; Cholesterol 223.5 mg; 3405 kJ (810 Cal)

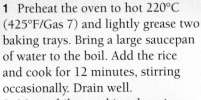

CHICKEN, ARTICHOKE AND BROAD BEAN STEW

Preparation time: 15 minutes
Cooking time: 1 hour 25 minutes
Serves 4

1 cup (155 g) frozen broad beans
8 chicken thighs on the bone (skin removed, optional)
1/2 cup (60 g) seasoned plain flour
2 tablespoons oil
1 large red onion, cut into small wedges
1/2 cup (125 ml) dry white wine
1 1/4 cups (310 ml) chicken stock
2 teaspoons finely chopped fresh rosemary
340 g marinated artichokes, well drained and quartered
800 potatoes, cut into large cubes
60 g butter

1 Remove the skins from the broad beans. Coat the chicken in the flour, shaking off the excess. Heat the oil in a saucepan or flameproof casserole dish, then brown the chicken in two batches on all sides over medium heat. Remove and drain on crumpled paper towels.
2 Add the onion to the pan and cook for 3–4 minutes, or until soft but not brown. Increase the heat to high, pour in the wine and boil for 2 minutes, or until reduced to a syrup. Stir in 1 cup (250 ml) of the stock and bring just to the boil, then return the chicken to the pan with the rosemary. Reduce the heat to low and simmer, covered, for 45 minutes.
3 Add the artichokes to the pan, increase the heat to high and return to the boil. Reduce to a simmer and cook, uncovered, for 10–15 minutes. Add the beans and cook for a further 5 minutes.
4 Meanwhile, cook the potato in a saucepan of boiling water for 15–20 minutes, or until tender. Drain, then return to the pan. Add the butter and the remaining stock and mash with a potato masher. Serve on the side of the stew.

NUTRITION PER SERVE
Fat 47 g; Protein 75.5 g; Carbohydrate 43 g; Dietary Fibre 8.5 g; Cholesterol 334 mg; 3845 kJ (920 Cal)

1

2

2

PAPRIKA VEAL WITH CARAWAY NOODLES

Preparation time: 10 minutes
Cooking time: 1 hour 35 minutes
Serves 4

3 tablespoons oil
1 kg veal shoulder, diced
1 large onion, thinly sliced
3 cloves garlic, finely chopped
1/4 cup (60 g) Hungarian paprika
1/2 teaspoon caraway seeds
2 x 400 g cans chopped tomatoes,
    one drained
350 g fresh fettuccine
40 g butter, softened

1 Heat half the oil in a large saucepan over medium–high heat, then brown the veal in batches for 3 minutes per batch. Remove the veal from the pan and set aside with any pan juices.

2 Add the remaining oil to the pan and sauté the onion and garlic over medium heat for 5 minutes, or until softened. Add the paprika and 1/4 teaspoon of the caraway seeds and stir for 30 seconds.

3 Add the chopped tomatoes and their liquid plus 1/2 cup (125 ml) water. Return the veal to the pan with any juices, increase the heat to high and bring to the boil. Reduce the heat to low, then cover and simmer for 1 hour 15 minutes, or until the meat is tender and the sauce has thickened.

4 About 15 minutes before the veal is ready, cook the pasta in a large saucepan of rapidly boiling salted water according to the packet instructions until *al dente*. Drain, then return to the pan. Stir in the butter and the remaining caraway seeds. Serve immediately with the paprika veal.

NUTRITION PER SERVE
Fat 25 g; Protein 67.5 g; Carbohydrate 73 g; Dietary Fibre 10 g; Cholesterol 230.5 mg; 3340 kJ (800 Cal)

1

3

EASY BAKES AND ROASTS

RACK OF PORK WITH FIG AND MARSALA SAUCE

Preparation time: 10 minutes +
  30 minutes soaking
Cooking time: 1 hour 40 minutes
Serves 4

300 g dessert figs, quartered
1/3 cup (80 ml) Marsala
2 teaspoons Dijon mustard
1/2 cup (125 ml) chicken stock
1.5 kg rack of pork, tied
120 ml oil
1 large red onion, sliced
18 fresh sage leaves
300 g beans, trimmed

1 Preheat the oven to very hot 240°C (475°F/Gas 9). Soak the figs, Marsala, mustard and stock for 30 minutes.
2 Score the rind of the pork in lines spaced 5 cm apart, brush with 2 tablespoons of the oil and season. Place in a large roasting tin, cook for 15 minutes, then reduce the heat to moderately hot 200°C (400°F/Gas 6). Add the onion, cook for 40 minutes, then add the fig mixture, cooking for 30–40 minutes, or until the pork juices run clear when the thickest section is pierced with a skewer.
3 Meanwhile, heat the remaining oil in a small saucepan over high heat. Add the sage leaves a few at a time for 30 seconds per batch. Remove with a slotted spoon and drain.
4 Remove the pork and onion pieces from the oven and allow the meat to rest for 5 minutes. Drain the excess fat from the roasting tin. Reduce the sauce on the stovetop for 5 minutes, stirring to scrape up any sediment stuck to the base of the pan.
5 Bring a saucepan of water to the boil, add the beans and cook for 4 minutes. Drain, season. Keep warm.
6 Slice the pork into portions, pour on the sauce and garnish with the sage leaves. Serve with the onions, beans and, if desired, mashed potato.

NUTRITION PER SERVE
Fat 28 g; Protein 51 g; Carbohydrate 20.5 g; Dietary Fibre 4 g; Cholesterol 142 mg; 2303 kJ (548 Cal)

CHICKEN AND LEEK PIES

Preparation time: 15 minutes +
  cooling
Cooking time: 1 hour
Serves 4

875 ml chicken and herb stock
4 chicken breasts
  (about 200 g each)
60 g butter
1 leek, thinly sliced
50 g plain flour
300 ml cream
1 cup (155 g) fresh or frozen peas,
  blanched
1 sheet ready-rolled puff pastry,
  thawed

1   Place the stock in a deep-sided frying pan then bring to the boil. Reduce the heat to medium–low so the liquid is just simmering, then gently poach the chicken for 10–12 minutes, or until just cooked (add 100 ml water if needed to keep the chicken covered). Allow to cool in the liquid. Remove the chicken, reserving the liquid, and cut into bite-sized pieces.

2   Melt the butter in a saucepan over medium heat and cook the leek for 5 minutes, or until soft. Add the flour and cook, stirring, until it starts to bubble. Stir in 1 cup (250 ml) of the reserved liquid and cook until it starts to thicken. Add the cream, reserving 1 tablespoon to glaze the pastry. Cook until the mixture just starts to boil. Stir in the chicken and the peas and cook for a further 5–6 minutes. Season. Remove from the heat and cool completely. Preheat the oven to moderately hot 200°C (400°F/Gas 6).

3   Divide the filling among four individual pie dishes or ramekins. Top with a circle of pastry, cut just bigger than the top of the dish, then press around the edges to seal. Brush the surface with the reserved cream. Place the dishes on a metal tray and bake for 20–25 minutes, or until the pastry is golden. Serve with a crisp green salad.

NUTRITION PER SERVE
Fat 65.5 g; Protein 53 g; Carbohydrate 31 g; Dietary Fibre 3.5 g; Cholesterol 284 mg; 3835 kJ (915 Cal)

1

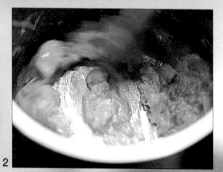

2

3

PORK LOIN ROAST WITH APPLE WALNUT STUFFING AND ROAST VEGETABLES

Preparation time: 15 minutes +
  10 minutes standing
Cooking time: 1 hour 30 minutes
Serves 4

½ cup (50 g) walnuts, chopped
1 green apple, peeled and cored
½ teaspoon ground cinnamon
2 tablespoons port
1.5 kg rindless, boned pork loin
100 ml maple syrup
8 parsnips, sliced thinly lengthways
500 g baby carrots
2 tablespoons oil

1 Preheat the oven to moderately hot 200°C (400°F/Gas 6). Grease a large roasting tin. Spread the walnuts on a baking tray and place under a medium–high grill for 2–3 minutes, or until lightly toasted.
2 Coarsely grate the apple and squeeze out the excess juice. Combine the apple, cinnamon, walnuts and port and season to taste.
3 Unroll the pork loin, then spread the stuffing evenly over one third of the loin lengthways. Re-roll the loin, tie securely and place, seam-side-down, in the prepared tin. Roast for 20 minutes. Reduce the heat to moderate 180°C (350°F/Gas 4), baste the pork with some maple syrup and roast for a further 30 minutes.
4 Toss together the parsnip, carrots and oil in a large bowl and season if necessary. Add to the roasting tin and roast for a further 30–35 minutes, or until the vegetables are golden and tender. In the last 10 minutes of cooking, baste the pork again with the syrup. Remove the roast pork from the tin, cover with foil and allow to rest for 10 minutes before slicing. Serve with the vegetables and any pan juices.

NUTRITION PER SERVE
Fat 31 g; Protein 67 g; Carbohydrate 48 g; Dietary Fibre 8.5 g; Cholesterol 179.5 mg; 3098 kJ (743 Cal)

COOK'S FILE
Variation: If you don't have port on hand, use 2 tablespoons apple cider.

2

3

3

BLUE EYE COD CUTLETS IN A SPICY TOMATO SAUCE

Preparation time: 5 minutes
Cooking time: 25 minutes
Serves 4

4 blue eye cod cutlets, 2.5 cm thick
   (about 250 g each)
1¼ cups (250 g) long-grain rice
2 tablespoons oil
1 teaspoon coriander seeds, lightly
   crushed
1 teaspoon black mustard seeds
1½ tablespoons sambal oelek
400 g can diced tomatoes
1 teaspoon garam masala
300 g baby English spinach leaves

1 Preheat the oven to moderate 180°C (350°F/Gas 4). Pat the cutlets dry with paper towels.
2 Bring a large saucepan of water to the boil. Add the rice and cook for 12 minutes, stirring occasionally. Drain well.
3 Meanwhile, heat 1 tablespoon of the oil in a saucepan over medium heat. When hot, add the coriander and mustard seeds—the mustard seeds should start to pop after about 30 seconds. Add the sambal oelek and cook for 30 seconds, then stir in the tomatoes and the garam masala. Bring to the boil, then reduce the heat to low and simmer, covered, for 6–8 minutes, or until the sauce thickens.
4 Heat the remaining oil in a large non-stick frying pan over medium heat. Add the cutlets and cook for 1 minute each side, or until evenly browned but not cooked through. Transfer to a 28 cm x 18.5 cm ceramic baking dish. Spoon the tomato sauce over the cutlets and bake for 10 minutes, or until the fish is cooked through.
5 Meanwhile, wash the spinach and put in a saucepan with just the water clinging to the leaves. Cook, covered, for 1 minute, or until the spinach has wilted. Serve the fish cutlets topped with sauce, with the spinach and some steamed rice.

NUTRITION PER SERVE
Fat 12 g; Protein 50.5 g; Carbohydrate 56 g; Dietary Fibre 4.5 g; Cholesterol 130 mg; 2245 kJ (535 Cal)

3

4

SAUSAGE AND BEAN HOT POT WITH ROASTED ORANGE SWEET POTATO

Preparation time: 15 minutes
Cooking time: 50 minutes
Serves 4

1 kg spicy Italian-style sausages
2 cloves garlic, roughly chopped
2 x 400 g cans cannellini beans
2 x 425 g cans crushed tomatoes
2 teaspoons Dijon mustard
750 g orange sweet potato, cut
    into 3 cm cubes
2 tablespoons olive oil
2 tablespoons coarsely chopped
    fresh parsley

1 Preheat the oven to moderately hot 200°C (400°F/Gas 6). Cook the sausages in a large frying pan over medium heat for 8–10 minutes, or until golden. Cut into 5 cm pieces and place in a 4 litre casserole dish. Add the garlic, beans, tomato, mustard and 2 tablespoons water to the dish and season with pepper. Stir well and cover with a lid. Place in the oven.

2 Meanwhile, toss the sweet potato with the oil and place snugly in a baking dish. Sprinkle with salt. Place in the oven with the casserole dish and bake for 25 minutes. Uncover the casserole dish and bake for a further 10–15 minutes, or until the hot pot is golden and bubbling and the sweet potato is soft and lightly golden brown. Serve the hot pot garnished with the parsley and the sweet potato on the side.

NUTRITION PER SERVE
Fat 66 g; Protein 46 g; Carbohydrate 59 g;
Dietary Fibre 18.5 g; Cholesterol 162.5 mg;
4185 kJ (1000 Cal)

COOK'S FILE
Hint: Make the hot pot up to 24 hours in advance and reheat to serve. You may need to add 1/2 cup (125 ml) water as it tends to thicken when refrigerated.

THAI GINGER FISH WITH CORIANDER BUTTER

Preparation time: 15 minutes
Cooking time: 10 minutes
Serves 4

60 g butter, at room temperature
1 tablespoon finely chopped fresh
　coriander leaves
2 tablespoons lime juice
1 tablespoon oil
1 tablespoon grated palm sugar
4 fresh long red chillies, seeded and
　chopped
2 stems lemon grass, trimmed
4 firm white fish fillets (blue eye cod
　or John Dory) (about 200 g each)
1 lime, thinly sliced
1 tablespoon finely shredded fresh
　ginger

1 Thoroughly mix the butter and coriander and roll it into a log. Wrap the log in plastic wrap and chill in the refrigerator until required.

2 Preheat the oven to moderately hot 200°C (400°F/Gas 6). Combine the lime juice, oil, palm sugar and chilli in a small non-metallic bowl and stir until the sugar has dissolved. Cut the lemon grass into halves.

3 Place a piece of lemon grass in the centre of a sheet of foil large enough to fully enclose one fillet. Place a fish fillet on top and smear the surface with the lime juice mixture. Top with some lime slices and ginger shreds, then wrap into a secure parcel. Repeat with the remaining ingredients to make four parcels.

4 Place the parcels in an ovenproof dish and bake for 8–10 minutes, or until the fish flakes easily when tested with a fork.

5 To serve, place the parcels on individual serving plates and serve open with slices of coriander butter, steamed rice and steamed greens.

NUTRITION PER SERVE
Fat 21.5 g; Protein 42 g; Carbohydrate 4.5 g; Dietary Fibre 1 g; Cholesterol 156.5 mg; 1590 kJ (380 Cal)

1

3

3

MOROCCAN ROAST LAMB WITH MINT COUSCOUS

Preparation time: 10 minutes +
    10 minutes resting
Cooking time: 1 hour 15 minutes
Serves 4

2 tablespoons olive oil
3 teaspoons ground cumin
3 teaspoons ground coriander
3 teaspoons sweet paprika
3 cloves garlic, crushed
1.5 kg easy-carve leg of lamb
1¹/₃ cups (245 g) couscous
2 tablespoons chopped fresh mint

1 Preheat the oven to moderate 180°C (350°F/Gas 4). Combine the oil, spices and 2 cloves crushed garlic to form a smooth paste. Season with salt and pepper. Rub a thick coating of the paste all over the lamb. Place on a rack in a roasting tin and roast for 1 hour 15 minutes, basting two or three times. Turn off the heat, leave the oven door ajar and allow to rest for 10 minutes.

2 Meanwhile, place the couscous in a heatproof bowl with 2 cups (500 ml) boiling water. Stir in the mint, the remaining garlic and ¹/₂ teaspoon salt. Cover and leave for 5 minutes, or until all the water has been absorbed, then gently fluff with a fork.

3 To serve, carve the lamb into thick slices and place on a bed of couscous. Pour the pan juices into a small jug and serve with the lamb. Garnish with fresh mint leaves, if desired.

NUTRITION PER SERVE
Fat 32.5 g; Protein 91 g; Carbohydrate 49 g; Dietary Fibre 2 g; Cholesterol 255 mg; 3575 kJ (855 Cal)

COOK'S FILE
Note: If roasted for 1 hour 15 minutes the lamb will be medium–well done. This gives good flavour right through the meat, while basting keeps it succulent.

1

MUSHROOM POT PIES

Preparation time: 15 minutes
Cooking time: 55 minutes
Serves 4

100 ml olive oil
1 leek, sliced
1 clove garlic, crushed
1 kg large field mushrooms, roughly
    chopped
1 teaspoon chopped fresh thyme
300 ml cream
1 sheet ready-rolled puff pastry,
    thawed
1 egg yolk, beaten, to glaze

1 Preheat the oven to moderate 180°C (350°F/Gas 4). Heat 1 tablespoon of the oil in a frying pan over medium heat. Cook the leek and garlic for 5 minutes, or until the leek is soft and translucent. Transfer to a large saucepan.

2 Heat the remaining oil in the frying pan over high heat and cook the mushrooms in two batches, stirring frequently, for 5–7 minutes per batch, or until the mushrooms have released their juices, are soft and slightly coloured. Transfer to the saucepan, then add the thyme.

3 Place the saucepan over high heat and stir in the cream until well mixed. Cook, stirring occasionally, for 7–8 minutes, or until the cream has reduced to a thick sauce. Remove from the heat and season well.

4 Divide the filling among four 1¼ cup (315 ml) ramekins or ovenproof bowls. Cut the pastry into rounds slightly larger than each dish. Brush the rim of the ramekins with a little of the egg yolk, place the pastry on top and press down to seal. Brush the top with the remaining egg yolk. Place the ramekins on a metal tray. Bake for 20–25 minutes, or until the pastry has risen and is golden brown. Great with mashed potato and a salad.

NUTRITION PER SERVE
Fat 65 g; Protein 13.5 g; Carbohydrate 20 g; Dietary Fibre 7.5 g; Cholesterol 158 mg; 2970 kJ (710 Cal)

COOK'S FILE
Variation: To make 1 large pie, transfer the filling to a 20 cm ceramic pie dish or 1.5 litre ovenproof dish. Brush the rim with a little egg yolk, place the pastry on top and press down to seal. Trim the pastry and decorate the centre with pastry shapes, if desired. Brush with the remaining egg yolk and bake for 30–35 minutes, or until golden brown.

1

2

3

RACK OF LAMB WITH MUSTARD CRUST AND PARSLEY POTATOES

Preparation time: 15 minutes
Cooking time: 45 minutes
Serves 4

2 racks of lamb (6 chops per rack),
    trimmed
1/4 cup (60 ml) oil
2 cups (160 g) fresh breadcrumbs
3 cloves garlic, chopped
1 teaspoon grated lemon rind
1/2 cup (10 g) fresh flat-leaf parsley,
    finely chopped
2 tablespoons tarragon Dijon mustard
150 g unsalted butter, softened
400 g baby new potatoes

1 Preheat the oven to hot 220°C (425°F/Gas 7). Score the fat side of the racks in a criss-cross pattern. Rub 1 tablespoon of the oil over the racks and season well. Heat the remaining oil in a frying pan over medium heat and cook the racks for 5–8 minutes, or until the surface is completely brown. Remove from the pan.

2 Combine the breadcrumbs, garlic, lemon rind and three quarters of the parsley. Add the mustard and 100 g of the butter to form a paste. Firmly press a layer of breadcrumb mixture over the fat side of the racks, then place in a roasting tin. Bake for 25 minutes, or until the breadcrumbs appear brown and crisp and the meat is cooked to medium. For well-done, continue to bake for 10 minutes, or until cooked to your liking. Cover the breadcrumb crust with foil to prevent it burning, if necessary.

3 About 25 minutes before the lamb is ready, toss the potatoes with the remaining butter until well coated. Season, then put in a roasting tin. Bake for 20 minutes, or until brown, then remove, sprinkle with the remaining parsley and season. To serve, cut the racks in half using the bones as a guide. Serve with the pan juices, potatoes and a tossed salad.

NUTRITION PER SERVE
Fat 53.5 g; Protein 43 g; Carbohydrate 41 g;
Dietary Fibre 4 g; Cholesterol 196.5 mg;
3420 kJ (815 Cal)

1

ROAST PEPPERED BEEF WITH ONIONS AND POTATOES

Preparation time: 15 minutes
Cooking time: 40 minutes
Serves 4

1 kg piece beef sirloin
2 tablespoons freshly ground black
    peppercorns
1 large red onion
4 large potatoes
50 g butter
1/4 cup (60 ml) beef stock
1/4 cup (60 ml) red wine
500 g mixed yellow and green beans

1 Preheat the oven to moderate 180°C (350°F/Gas 4). Trim the excess fat from the beef, leaving a thin layer. Press the pepper all over the beef.

2 Cut the onion and potatoes into 5 mm thick slices and place in a roasting tin. Sit the beef on top, fat-side-up. Cut 40 g of the butter into small pieces and dot all over the beef and potatoes. Pour in the stock and wine and bake for 35–40 minutes, for medium–rare, or until cooked to your liking. Remove the beef from the oven and rest for at least 5 minutes before carving.

3 Meanwhile, bring a saucepan of lightly salted water to the boil. Add the mixed beans and cook for 2–4 minutes, or until just tender. Drain well, then add the remaining butter and toss together. Keep warm until ready to serve.

4 To serve, divide the onion and potato mixture among four serving plates and top with slices of beef. Spoon on any pan juices and serve with the beans.

NUTRITION PER SERVE
Fat 26 g; Protein 59 g; Carbohydrate 29 g; Dietary Fibre 6.5 g; Cholesterol 177 mg; 2510 kJ (600 Cal)

2

VEGETABLE BAKE

Preparation time: 15 minutes
Cooking time: 1 hour
Serves 4

400 g potatoes, thinly sliced
   lengthways
60 g butter, melted
1½–2 teaspoons finely chopped
   fresh thyme
400 g pumpkin, thinly sliced
300 g zucchini, thinly sliced
   lengthways
1 cup (250 ml) Italian tomato passata
½ cup (50 g) grated Parmesan

1 Preheat the oven to warm 170°C (325°F/Gas 3). Grease a 1.5 litre rectangular ovenproof dish. Combine the potato with one third each of the butter and thyme. Season, then place in the base of the prepared dish.
2 Combine the pumpkin and another third of the butter and thyme. Season and press onto the potato. Combine the zucchini with the remaining butter and thyme. Season and press on to the pumpkin.
3 Spread the passata evenly over the top and cover with a piece of greased foil. Bake for 45 minutes, remove the foil and sprinkle with the grated Parmesan. Bake for a further 15 minutes, or until the top is golden brown and the vegetables are cooked through. Serve with a salad and crusty bread, if desired.

NUTRITION PER SERVE
Fat 16.5 g; Protein 12 g; Carbohydrate 28 g; Dietary Fibre 7 g; Cholesterol 48.5 mg; 1305 kJ (310 Cal)

2

3

ARTICHOKE, OLIVE AND GOAT'S CHEESE PIZZA

Preparation time: 10 minutes
Cooking time: 20 minutes
Serves 4

25 cm purchased pizza base
1/3 cup (80 ml) Italian tomato passata
150 g marinated artichokes,
    quartered
70 g pitted Kalamata olives
1 clove garlic, thinly sliced
50 g goat's cheese, crumbled
good-quality olive oil, to drizzle
2 tablespoons chopped fresh
    oregano

1 Preheat the oven to hot 220°C (425°F/Gas 7). Place the pizza base on a baking tray, then spread with the tomato passata. Evenly scatter the artichoke pieces, olives and the garlic over the passata, then top with the crumbled goat's cheese.
2 Lightly drizzle the surface of the pizza with olive oil and bake for 20 minutes, or until golden. Sprinkle with fresh oregano and season with salt and freshly ground black pepper. Cut into wedges and serve.

NUTRITION PER SERVE
Fat 10 g; Protein 10.5 g; Carbohydrate 50 g; Dietary Fibre 5.5 g; Cholesterol 6 mg; 1390 kJ (335 Cal)

1

SHEPHERD'S PIE WITH GARLIC MASH

Preparation time: 15 minutes
Cooking time: 1 hour 40 minutes
Serves 4

1 1/2 tablespoons oil
1 large onion, finely chopped
1 carrot, finely diced
8 garlic cloves, peeled
750 g lean lamb mince
1 1/2 cups (375 ml) Italian tomato
    passata
300 ml beef stock
800 g potatoes, cut into large chunks
30 g butter

1 Heat the oil in a large saucepan over medium heat. Add the onion and carrot, and cook for 5 minutes, or until softened. Crush 2 garlic cloves and sauté with the onion mixture for another minute. Add the lamb mince and stir well, breaking up any lumps with the back of a wooden spoon. Cook for 5 minutes, or until browned and cooked through. Drain off any excess fat with a large spoon, then add the tomato passata and 1 cup (250 ml) of the stock. Cover and bring to the boil. Reduce the heat to medium–low and simmer for 25 minutes. Uncover and cook for a further 20 minutes, or until the sauce reduces and thickens. Preheat the oven to moderately hot 200°C (400°F/Gas 6).

2 Meanwhile, place the potato in a saucepan of boiling water with the remaining garlic and cook for 15–20 minutes, or until tender. Drain well, then return to the pan over low heat, stirring to evaporate any excess water. Remove the pan from the heat, add the butter and the remaining stock and mash until smooth. Season.

3 Transfer the lamb mixture to a 1.5 litre ovenproof ceramic dish. Spoon the mashed potato over the top and spread it out evenly. Use a fork to swirl the surface. Bake for 40 minutes, or until the potato is golden brown.

NUTRITION PER SERVE
Fat 27 g; Protein 48.5 g; Carbohydrate 42 g; Dietary Fibre 9.5 g; Cholesterol 148.5 mg; 2545 kJ (610 Cal)

COOK'S FILE
Ahead of time: The lamb mixture can be made the day before and refrigerated or in advance and frozen until required.

1

2

BAKED MEDITERRANEAN PORK CUTLETS

Preparation time: 15 minutes +
   20 minutes marinating
Cooking time: 45 minutes
Serves 4

4 large pork loin cutlets, trimmed
2 tablespoons olive oil
2 cloves garlic, finely chopped
1 tablespoon finely chopped fresh
   rosemary
2 tablespoons fresh thyme
2 tablespoons balsamic vinegar
4 Roma tomatoes, halved lengthways
1 large red capsicum
4 small zucchini, trimmed and halved
   lengthways

1 Preheat the oven to hot 220°C (425°F/Gas 7) and lightly grease a baking tin. Arrange the pork cutlets in a single layer in the tin. Combine the olive oil, garlic, rosemary, thyme and 1 tablespoon of the balsamic vinegar, then spoon half the mixture over the pork cutlets. Season to taste with salt and black pepper. Cover with plastic wrap and marinate for 20 minutes.

2 Place 2 tomato halves, cut-side-down, on each cutlet and sprinkle the tomatoes with the remaining balsamic vinegar.

3 Remove the seeds from the capsicum and cut into 2 cm strips. Toss the capsicum and zucchini with the remaining herb mixture, then add to the dish around the cutlets.

Bake for 45 minutes, or until cooked through and well browned. Season to taste. Serve the cutlets with the roast vegetables, a green salad and crusty bread.

NUTRITION PER SERVE
Fat 17.5 g; Protein 42.5 g; Carbohydrate 4 g; Dietary Fibre 2.5 g; Cholesterol 116 mg; 1450 kJ (345 Cal)

3

RUSTIC GREEK PIE

Preparation time: 15 minutes
Cooking time: 30 minutes
Serves 4

450 g packet frozen spinach, thawed
1 large sheet ready-rolled shortcrust
    pastry, thawed
3 cloves garlic, finely chopped
150 g haloumi, grated
120 g feta, crumbled
1 tablespoon fresh oregano sprigs
2 eggs
¼ cup (60 ml) cream
lemon wedges, to serve

1 Preheat the oven to moderately hot 200°C (400°F/Gas 6). Squeeze the excess liquid from the spinach.

2 Place the pastry on a baking tray and spread the spinach in the middle, leaving a 3 cm border around the edge. Sprinkle the garlic over the spinach and pile the haloumi and feta on top. Sprinkle with oregano and season well. Cut a short slit into each corner of the pastry, then tuck each side of pastry over to form a border around the filling.

3 Lightly beat the eggs with the cream and carefully pour the egg mixture over the spinach filling. Bake for 25–30 minutes, or until the pastry is golden and the filling is set. Serve with the lemon wedges and a fresh green salad.

NUTRITION PER SERVE
Fat 35 g; Protein 24 g; Carbohydrate 21 g;
Dietary Fibre 6.5 g; Cholesterol 176 mg;
2050 kJ (490 Cal)

1

2

ROAST LEMON CHICKEN WITH BAKED VEGETABLES

Preparation time: 15 minutes
Cooking time: 1 hour 20 minutes
Serves 4

1.5 kg whole chicken
75 ml lemon juice
1/2 lemon
9 cloves garlic, whole and unpeeled
1/3 cup (80 ml) olive oil
1 kg roasting potatoes, cut into
    5 cm pieces
4 red onions, cut into quarters
8 small zucchini, trimmed and cut
    in half lengthways
1 cup (250 ml) chicken stock

1 Preheat the oven to hot 220°C (425°F/Gas 7). Wash the chicken and pat dry inside and out with paper towels, then place in a large roasting tin. Pour 25 ml of the lemon juice over the chicken, then place the lemon half and 1 clove garlic inside the chicken cavity. Brush the outside with 1 tablespoon of the oil. Season.
2 Arrange the potato and remaining garlic cloves around the chicken. Brush the potatoes with 2 tablespoons of the oil and roast for 20 minutes. Reduce the heat to moderately hot 190°C (375°F/Gas 5). Place the onion around the chicken, turning the potatoes at the same time. Return to the oven for a further 30 minutes.
3 Place the zucchini cut-side-down on a baking tray and brush with the remaining oil, then place in the oven. Baste the chicken with its pan juices and pour the remaining lemon juice over the top. Turn the onion and potatoes and roast for 20 minutes, or until the chicken is golden and the juices run clear when pierced between the breast and thigh.
4 Transfer the chicken, potatoes, garlic and onion to a serving plate, cover with foil and keep warm for 10 minutes. Check the zucchini halves are tender and nicely coloured—they may need to stay in the oven.
5 Meanwhile, to make the gravy, place the roasting tin over high heat and add the chicken stock. Stir with a wooden spoon to scrape up any sediment and boil for 7–8 minutes, or until it reduces and thickens.
6 To serve, remove the lemon and garlic from the cavity and discard. Serve the chicken with the onion, garlic, zucchini, potatoes and gravy.

NUTRITION PER SERVE
Fat 41 g; Protein 45 g; Carbohydrate 57 g; Dietary Fibre 10 g; Cholesterol 160 mg; 3255 kJ (775 Cal)

MUSTARD CRUSTED SCOTCH FILLET WITH ROAST VEGETABLES

Preparation time: 15 minutes +
    10 minutes resting
Cooking time: 1 hour
Serves 4

16 French shallots
½ cup (125 g) wholegrain mustard
3 cloves garlic, crushed
1.2–1.5 kg scotch fillet
200 g parsnips, cut into 2 cm chunks
400 g potatoes, cut lengthways into
    wedges
200 g orange sweet potato, cut into
    wedges
⅓ cup (80 ml) olive oil

1 Preheat the oven to moderately hot 200°C (400°F/Gas 6). Peel four of the French shallots, slice into thick rings and arrange them in the centre of a large roasting tin.

2 Combine the mustard and garlic, and season well with salt and pepper. Rub the mixture over the surface of the beef, then place the beef on top of the sliced shallots. Toss the parsnip, potato, sweet potato, the remaining shallots, and ¼ cup (60 ml) of the oil together, then arrange around the beef. Drizzle the remaining oil over the beef and roast for 30 minutes.

3 Season and turn the vegetables—don't worry if some of the mustard mixes through. Roast for a further 30 minutes for a medium–rare result, or until cooked to your liking. Turn the oven off, leave the door ajar and allow to rest for 10 minutes.

4 To serve, carve the beef and spoon the pan juices on the top. Serve with the roasted vegetables, whole shallots, and some steamed greens, if desired.

NUTRITION PER SERVE
Fat 34 g; Protein 77.5 g; Carbohydrate 29 g;
Dietary Fibre 6 g; Cholesterol 226 mg;
3038 kJ (728 Cal)

2

2

BALSAMIC ROASTED VEAL CUTLETS WITH RED ONION

Preparation time: 10 minutes
Cooking time: 45 minutes
Serves 4

1½ tablespoons olive oil
8 veal cutlets
4 cloves garlic, unpeeled
1 red onion, cut into thin wedges
1 tablespoon chopped fresh
    rosemary
250 g cherry tomatoes
¼ cup (60 ml) balsamic vinegar
2 teaspoons soft brown sugar
2 tablespoons chopped fresh
    flat-leaf parsley

1 Preheat the oven to moderately hot 200°C (400°F/Gas 6). Heat the oil in a large frying pan over medium heat. Cook the cutlets in batches for 4 minutes on both sides, or until brown.

2 Arrange the cutlets in a single layer in a large, shallow-sided roasting tin. Add the garlic, onion, rosemary, tomatoes, vinegar and sugar. Season well with salt and freshly ground black pepper.

3 Cover tightly with foil and roast for 15 minutes. Remove the foil and roast for a further 10–15 minutes, depending on the thickness of the veal chops.

4 Transfer the cutlets, garlic, onion and tomatoes to serving plates. Stir the pan juices and spoon over the top. Garnish with the chopped parsley and serve immediately. Delicious with a creamy garlic mash and a tossed green salad.

NUTRITION PER SERVE
Fat 11 g; Protein 41 g; Carbohydrate 5 g; Dietary Fibre 2 g; Cholesterol 146 mg; 1200 kJ (285 Cal)

1

AROMATIC SNAPPER PARCELS

Preparation time: 10 minutes
Cooking time: 20 minutes
Serves 4

1 cup (30 g) loosely packed fresh
    basil leaves, chopped
2 large cloves garlic, chopped
1 tablespoon lemon juice
1 teaspoon grated lemon rind
1/4 cup (60 ml) olive oil
4 skinless snapper fillets, trimmed
    and boned (about 200 g each)
500 g small new potatoes
20 asparagus spears
12 yellow baby squash

1 Preheat the oven to moderately hot 200°C (400°F/Gas 6). Combine the basil, garlic, lemon juice, rind and 2 tablespoons of the olive oil. Season to taste.

2 Place a fish fillet in the centre of a sheet of foil large enough to fully enclose it. Season. Smear the fillet with 2 teaspoons of the basil mixture, then wrap into a secure parcel. Repeat with the remaining fillets. Place on a baking tray and refrigerate until required.

3 Cook the potatoes in a large saucepan of boiling water for 15–20 minutes, or until tender. Drain and keep warm. While the potatoes are cooking, brush the asparagus and squash with the remaining oil. Place on a baking tray and season with freshly ground black pepper. Bake for 8–10 minutes, or until golden and tender.

4 About 10 minutes before the vegetables are ready, place the fish parcels in the oven and cook for 5–7 minutes, or until the flesh flakes easily when tested with a fork. Check one of the parcels after 5 minutes to see if the fish is cooked through.

5 Place the opened parcels on serving plates with the vegetables, season to taste and serve.

NUTRITION PER SERVE
Fat 17 g; Protein 49 g; Carbohydrate 22 g;
Dietary Fibre 7 g; Cholesterol 122 mg;
1845 kJ (440 Cal)

COOK'S FILE
Variation: Use ling or tail pieces of salmon fillet instead of the snapper.

2

4

TORTILLA PIE

Preparation time: 15 minutes
Cooking time: 25 minutes
Serves 4

1 tablespoons oil
500 g lean beef mince
35 g packet taco seasoning mix
420 g can Mexican chilli beans,
    drained
8 flour tortillas
2 cups (250 g) grated Cheddar
300 g Mexican tomato salsa
150 g sour cream
1 avocado, diced

1   Preheat the oven to moderate 180°C (350°F/Gas 4). Grease a 23 cm pie dish. Heat the oil in a large non-stick frying pan. Add the mince and cook for 5 minutes, or until brown, breaking up the lumps with the back of a spoon. Drain off the excess oil. Add the seasoning mix and cook for 5 minutes. Stir in the beans until heated through.

2   Lay a tortilla in the base of the pie dish, then spread 1/2 cup (125 g) of the mince mixture on top. Sprinkle with 1/4 cup (30 g) cheese and 1 tablespoon salsa. Continue layering with the remaining tortillas, mince mixture, cheese and salsa, ending with a tortilla sprinkled with a little cheese—it should end up looking like a dome shape.

3   Bake for 15 minutes, or until all the cheese has melted and browned. Cool slightly, cut into wedges and top with a dollop of sour cream and the diced avocado. Serve with a tomato salad, if desired.

NUTRITION PER SERVE
Fat 63 g; Protein 52 g; Carbohydrate 40.5 g;
Dietary Fibre 9 g; Cholesterol 173.5 mg;
3915 kJ (938 Cal)

2

3

MEXICAN CHICKEN BAKE

Preparation time: 15 minutes
Cooking time: 1 hour
Serves 4

3/4 cup (165 g) short-grain rice
300 g can red kidney beans, drained
    and thoroughly rinsed
3 1/2 tablespoons chopped fresh
    coriander leaves
1 tablespoon oil
600 g boneless, skinless chicken
    thigh fillets, unrolled
2 x 200 g jars spicy taco sauce
2 cups (250 g) grated Cheddar
1/2 cup (125 g) sour cream

1 Preheat the oven to moderate 180°C (350°F/Gas 4). Lightly grease a deep (7 cm) round (21 cm) ceramic casserole dish. Bring a large saucepan of water to the boil, add the rice and cook for 10–12 minutes, stirring occasionally. Drain.
2 In the prepared dish, combine the beans and 1 1/2 tablespoons of the coriander, then add the rice and toss together. Lightly press the mixture so the beans are mixed into the rice and the mixture is flat.
3 Heat the oil in a large frying pan over medium–high heat. Sauté the chicken thighs for 3 minutes, then turn over. Add the spicy taco sauce, and cook for a further 3 minutes.
4 To assemble, spread half the cheese over the rice. Arrange the thighs and sauce on top in a star shape, sprinkle with 1 1/2 tablespoons of the coriander, then sprinkle with the remaining cheese. Cover with foil.
5 Bake for 35–40 minutes, or until the mixture is bubbling and the cheese is melted and slightly browned—remove the foil for the last 5 minutes of cooking. Cut into four servings with a knife and scoop out carefully, keeping the layers intact. Serve sprinkled with the remaining coriander and a dollop of sour cream.

NUTRITION PER SERVE
Fat 49.5 g; Protein 52 g; Carbohydrate 66 g; Dietary Fibre 6 g; Cholesterol 234.5 mg; 3825 kJ (915 Cal)

DESSERTS

DURING THE WEEK, DESSERT IS USUALLY ABANDONED BECAUSE OF THE EXTRA TIME IT TAKES
TO PREPARE, BUT THESE HOT AND COLD SWEETS TAKE LITTLE TIME AT ALL.

CHOCOLATE CHERRY PARFAIT

chocolate ice cream (1–2 scoops each) • 400 g can pitted
black cherries, drained • lamington or choc-chip flavoured
ice cream (1–2 scoops each) • 1/3 cup (80 ml) good-quality
chocolate sauce • dark chocolate cherry bar, chopped,
to garnish

Divide the chocolate ice cream, cherries and lamington
ice cream among four parfait glasses. Drizzle with
the chocolate sauce and garnish with the
chocolate cherry bar. Serve at once.
Serves 4.

BANANA CARAMEL ICE CREAM STACK

400 g pound cake, cut into 1.5 cm thick slices (you will
need eight slices) • 4 rectangular slabs vanilla ice cream •
2 large bananas, cut on the diagonal into 1 cm slices •
3 tablespoons good-quality caramel sauce, plus extra to
drizzle • 1/3 cup (50 g) honey-roasted macadamia nuts,
chopped, plus extra, to garnish

Place a slice of cake on each of four serving plates, then
top each slice with an ice cream slab. Divide the banana
slices, caramel sauce and chopped nuts among each
serving, then top with another slice of cake. Drizzle with
extra caramel sauce and scatter with the extra nuts. Serve
immediately. Serves 4.

Note: Any unused cake can be frozen.

INDIVIDUAL MANGO PASSIONFRUIT TRIFLES

60 g plain sponge cake, cut into 1 cm pieces •
2 tablespoons Cointreau • 2 small or 1 large mango, cut
into bite-sized slices • 2 tablespoons passionfruit pulp •
1/2 cup (125 ml) ready-made vanilla custard • 200 g
mascarpone • 1 tablespoon icing sugar • passionfruit
pulp, extra, to garnish (optional)

Divide the cake pieces among four tall glasses (about
1 1/4 cups/310 ml). Drizzle 2 teaspoons Cointreau over
the cake in each glass, then leave for 5 minutes. Arrange
half the mango on the cake. Divide the passionfruit pulp
and custard evenly among the glasses, then top with the
remaining mango slices. Gently combine the mascarpone
and icing sugar until light and creamy. Just before
serving, dollop the marscapone mixture on top and
garnish with extra passionfruit. Serve at once. Serves 4.

Note: Another 1–2 tablespoons of custard can replace the
layer of mascarpone, if preferred.

MELON WITH LEMON GRASS SYRUP

1/4 cup (60 g) caster sugar • 3 fresh kaffir lime leaves •
2 lemon grass stems (white part only), bruised • 2 thin
slices fresh ginger • 250 g watermelon, seeded and
peeled • 250 g honeydew melon • 250 g rockmelon •
12 lychees, peeled

Heat the sugar and 1 cup (250 ml) water in a small
saucepan over medium heat and stir until the sugar has
dissolved. Add the lime leaves, lemon grass and ginger,
and simmer rapidly for 5–7 minutes, or until thickened.
Cool completely. Cut each melon into 2 cm cubes, then
place in a large bowl with the lychees. Discard the lime
leaves, lemon grass and ginger from the syrup. Pour the
syrup over the fruit and serve with vanilla ice cream, if
desired. Serves 4.

Hint: The longer the fruit sits in the syrup, the better—the
flavours will develop as the fruit becomes infused with the
syrup. It will store well for up to 3 days in the refrigerator.

LIME DELICIOUS PUDDING

1/4 cup (60 g) butter, softened • 1/3 cup (90 g) caster sugar • 3 eggs, separated • 1 1/2 teaspoons finely grated lime rind • 1/4 cup (30 g) self-raising flour • 3/4 cup (185 ml) milk • 1/4 cup (60 ml) lime juice • icing sugar, to dust

Preheat the oven to moderate 180°C (350°F/Gas 4) and lightly grease four 1 cup (250 ml) ramekins. Beat the butter, sugar, egg yolks and lime rind with electric beaters until light and creamy. Fold the flour into the mixture in two batches, alternating with the milk and lime juice. Beat the egg whites in a clean, dry bowl, until just stiff, then lightly fold into the pudding mixture until just combined. Spoon into the prepared ramekins and place into a large, deep baking tray. Pour in enough water to come halfway up the side of the ramekins and bake for 25 minutes, or until risen and golden on top. Dust lightly with icing sugar and serve at once. Serves 4.

CHOCOLATE CROISSANT PUDDING

3 eggs • 1/4 cup (60 g) caster sugar • 1 1/4 cups (310 ml) milk • 3 plain croissants, torn into small pieces • 100 g rum and raisin dark chocolate, roughly chopped • 1 tablespoon mixed peel • 1 tablespoon demerara sugar

Preheat the oven to moderate 180°C (350°F/Gas 4). Grease a 1.25 litre rectangular ovenproof dish. Whisk the eggs and sugar together until the sugar dissolves, then whisk in the milk until combined and frothy. Place half the croissants in the prepared dish, scatter the chocolate and mixed peel on top, then pour on half the egg mixture. Repeat with the remaining croissant pieces and egg mixture. Sprinkle the surface with the demerara sugar. Place the dish in a large deep baking tray. Pour in enough water to come halfway up the sides of the dish and bake for 40–45 minutes, or until set and golden on top. Serve with ice cream. Serves 4–6.

APPLE CRUMBLE

6 apples, peeled, cored and finely sliced • 2 cinnamon sticks • 2 cm x 4 cm piece lemon rind • 1/3 cup (60 g) soft brown sugar • 50 g chopped unsalted butter • 1/2 cup (60 g) plain flour • 2 tablespoons flaked almonds

Preheat the oven to moderately hot 200°C (400°F/Gas 6). Lightly grease a 1.25 litre ovenproof dish. Place the apple, cinnamon sticks, lemon rind, 1 tablespoon of the brown sugar, and 1/2 cup (125 ml) water in a large saucepan. Simmer, partially covered, over medium heat for 8–10 minutes, or until the apple is tender but still holding its shape. Discard the cinnamon and lemon rind. Transfer the apple mixture to the prepared dish. Mix the plain flour, 40 g of the butter and 2 tablespoons of the brown sugar in a small bowl with your fingertips, rubbing in the butter until it resembles coarse breadcrumbs. Mix in the almonds until well coated. Sprinkle the crumble mixture over the apples, then scatter the remaining butter and soft brown sugar on top. Bake for 15 minutes, or until golden brown. Serve hot or cold, with custard or ice cream. Serves 4.

CHERRY GALETTES

2 sheets ready-rolled puff pastry • 200 g cream cheese, softened • 1 tablespoon grated lemon rind • 670 g jar morello cherries, drained • 1/4 cup (80 g) sour cherry jam, melted • thick cream, to serve

Preheat the oven to moderately hot 200°C (400°F/Gas 6). Cut two rounds (14 cm diameter) from each sheet of pastry. Prick each round several times with a fork and place on a large baking tray. Bake for 5 minutes, then cool slightly. Mix the cream cheese and lemon rind together, then divide among the pastry rounds, spreading to leave a 2 cm border around the edge of the pastry. Arrange about 1/3 cup (65 g) cherries on each round, and brush the surface with the melted jam. Bake for 20 minutes, or until the pastry is puffed and golden. Serve hot with a dollop of thick cream. Serves 4.

Note: Any remaining cherries will last in the refrigerator for up to a week—use them in the Chocolate Cherry Parfait on page 106.

INDEX

First published by Murdoch Books Pty Limited,
Erico House, 6th Floor, 93-99 Upper Richmond Road, Putney, London SW15 2TG

Editorial Director: Diana Hill
Editor: Stephanie Kistner
Creative Director: Marylouise Brammer
Designer: Wing Ping Tong
Food Director: Jane Lawson
Food Editor: Kathleen Gandy
Recipe Development: Alison Adams, Rekha Arnott, Jane Charlton, Rebecca Clancy,
Judy Clarke, Michelle Earl, Justin Finlay, Kathleen Gandy, Joanne Glynn,
Sonia Greig, Jane Griffiths, Fiona Hammond, David Herbert, Kathy Knudsen,
Jane Lawson, Valli Little, Barbara Lowery, Kate Murdoch, Kim Passenger, Sarah Randell,
Jo Richardson, John Skinner, Jennifer Tolhurst, Angela Tregonning
Home Economists: Alison Adams, Rekha Arnott, Justin Finlay, Valli Little, Angela Tregonning
Photographer: Ian Hofstetter
Food Stylist: Marie-Hélène Clauzon
Food Preparation: Angela Tregonning
Nutritionist: Dr Susanna Holt

Chief Executive: Juliet Rogers
Publisher: Kay Scarlett

ISBN 978 1 74196 047 1

This edition published 2007 for Index Books Ltd,
Garrard Way, Kettering, Northants, NN16 8TD.

Printed by 1010 Printing International Limited. PRINTED IN CHINA.

Copyright© Text, design, photography and illustrations Murdoch Books 2002.
All rights reserved. No part of this publication may be reproduced, stored in a retrieval system
or transmitted in any form or by any means, electronic, mechanical, photocopying,
recording or otherwise without the prior written permission of the publisher.

INTERNATIONAL GLOSSARY OF INGREDIENTS

capsicum	red or green pepper	fresh coriander	fresh cilantro
eggplant	aubergine	puréed tomato (Aus.)	sieved crushed tomatoes/
tomato paste (Aus.)	tomato purée, double		passata (UK)
	concentrate (UK)	zucchini	courgette